Morton Feldman's
Piano and String Quartet

Morton Feldman's
Piano and String Quartet

Analysis, Aesthetics, and Experience of a 20th-Century Masterpiece

Ray Fields

ROWMAN & LITTLEFIELD
Lanham • Boulder • New York • London

Published by Rowman & Littlefield
An imprint of The Rowman & Littlefield Publishing Group, Inc.
4501 Forbes Boulevard, Suite 200, Lanham, Maryland 20706
www.rowman.com

86-90 Paul Street, London, EC2A 4NE

Copyright © 2022 by The Rowman & Littlefield Publishing Group, Inc.
All examples, except Figures 1.1 and 1.2, are from the score of the *Piano and String Quartet: Morton Feldman Piano and String Quartet* © Copyright 1985 by Universal Edition (London) Ltd., London/UE17972 (used with permission) www.universaledition.com.
Figures 1.1 and 1.2 are published and copyrighted by C. F. Peters.

All rights reserved. No part of this book may be reproduced in any form or by any electronic or mechanical means, including information storage and retrieval systems, without written permission from the publisher, except by a reviewer who may quote passages in a review.

British Library Cataloguing in Publication Information Available

Library of Congress Cataloging-in-Publication Data

Names: Fields, Ray, 1945– author.
Title: Morton Feldman's Piano and string quartet : analysis, aesthetics, and experience of a 20th-century masterpiece / Ray Fields.
Description: Lanham : Lexington Books, 2022. | Includes bibliographical references and index. | Summary: "Written in 1985, the year before Feldman's death, this single movement, 79-minute composition is heralded by many to be the composer's crowning achievement. The book is a complete analysis of the work, including the aural experience, and features interviews with notable Feldman performers: David Harrington of the Kronos Quartet and Aki Takahashi"— Provided by publisher.
Identifiers: LCCN 2022020024 (print) | LCCN 2022020025 (ebook) | ISBN 9781538172278 (cloth) | ISBN 9781538196397 (pbk.) | ISBN 9781538172285 (ebook)
Subjects: LCSH: Feldman, Morton, 1926–1987. Piano and string quartet.
Classification: LCC ML410.F2957 F54 2022 (print) | LCC ML410.F2957 (ebook) | DDC 780.92—dc23/eng/20220505
LC record available at https://lccn.loc.gov/2022020024
LC ebook record available at https://lccn.loc.gov/2022020025

For my wife Sharon,
who makes everything possible.

"Never expected to write a piece with just broken chords!"
—Morton Feldman, Letter to Aki Takahashi, September 11, 1985

Contents

Acknowledgments		ix
1	Introduction	1
2	Analytical Approach	19
3	Large-scale Structure of *Piano and String Quartet*	35
4	Detailed Analysis of Part A	45
5	Detailed Analysis of Part B	67
6	Part C—Repetition, Variance, Stasis	79
7	Conclusion—The Sonic Experience of *Piano and String Quartet*	91
Appendix A: Key for Locating Measures in the Score of *Piano and String Quartet*		99
Appendix B: Photocopy of Letter from Morton Feldman to Aki Takahashi, Most Likely September 11, 1985		103
Appendix C: Selected Bibliography: Analytical Studies of the Music of Morton Feldman		105
Appendix D: Interview with David Harrington		111
Appendix E: Page from Morton Feldman's Sketches for *Piano and String Quartet*		119

Selected Bibliography	121
Index	123
About the Author	125

Acknowledgments

I would like to express gratitude to and recognize the many individuals whose contributions were invaluable in carrying out this study of Morton Feldman's *Piano and String Quartet*.

David Harrington of the Kronos Quartet and pianist Aki Takahashi were long-time friends and colleagues of Feldman who premiered *Piano and String Quartet* under the composer's supervision and recorded it; they provided insights about Feldman, the composition's inception, and apparent errors and ambiguities in the autograph score.

David Felder, Ursula Oppens, and Christos Hatzis shared first-person memories about Feldman the man and composer.

Thomas Moore and David Lassus described the experience of Feldman's music from the performer's perspective.

Douglas Boyce, Matthew Chung, Bradley Green, and Christopher Newman participated in the cognitive research on the aural experience of *Piano and String Quartet*.

Felix Meyer, director of the Paul Sacher *Stiftung,* and staff members Isolde Ott Degen, Sabine Hänggi, Carlos Chanfón, and Heidrun Ziems lent their considerable expertise to the author in exploring the depths of the Feldman Archive.

Mark DeVoto was a source of sage advice and provided a close reading of the text as it came to completion.

Thanks to Michael Tan and Amelia Manasterli of Rowman & Littlefield for their keen guidance, ready support, and thoughtful responsiveness.

Most of all, thanks go to Thomas DeLio, mentor, friend, and Feldman scholar, whose support of this study and clarity of expression are a continuing inspiration.

Chapter One

Introduction

"I could die very happily, now that I wrote the *Piano and String Quartet*."[1]

In July 1986, the year before his death, American composer Morton Feldman gave a series of lectures at the festival "Nieuwe Muziek" in Middelburg in the Netherlands. Feldman had often used ambiguous language, metaphors, and references to extraneous influences when talking about his music and approach to composition.

> I'm very *into* acoustical reality. For me, there is no such thing as a compositional reality.[2]

> My music is handmade, so I'm like a tailor. I make my button holes by hand. The suit fits better.[3]

> There was a period—*The Rothko Chapel, The Viola in My Life* (1970–71), a few other pieces—when I was thinking of Bob Rauschenberg's photo montages. At that time, I would use a tune just the way Bob would put a photo on a canvas.[4]

But in speaking about *Piano and String Quartet* in his lecture "Doing it one way and doing it another way" at the festival on July 6, 1986, Feldman was remarkably explicit in his comments about a work he had completed the previous September.

> There are some pieces that for whatever reason . . . are very close to you . . . I've written hundreds and hundreds of pieces. The *Piano and String Quartet* has become my favorite piece in my whole life. . . . It has everything I ever wanted.[5]

What was "everything [Feldman] ever wanted?" He had spent his life as a composer asking and addressing fundamental questions about the nature of music, attempting to free himself—and his music—from the controlling yoke of what he termed "systems" and "procedures" that had evolved throughout music history. As he saw it:

> Of course, the history of music has always been involved with controls, rarely with any new sensitivity to sound. Whatever breakthroughs have occurred, took place only when new systems were devised. The systems extended music's vocabulary, but in essence were nothing more than complex ways of saying the same things. Music is still based on just a few technical models. As soon as you leave them you are in an area of music not recognizable as such.[6]

> . . . controls can be thought of as nothing more than accepted practice.[7]

> And the biggest problem in music is how you do it without a process. And the unbelievable vested interest in the history of musical process. Process in the sense that to some degree is not involved in any kind of acoustical reality.[8]

Ultimately, it was that "new sensitivity to sound" that Feldman sought. He was "desirous of a sound world more direct, more immediate, more physical than anything that had existed heretofore."[9] As Feldman scholar Thomas DeLio has written,

> From his earliest graphic scores to his late, very long compositions, Morton Feldman remained constant in his attempt to convey the immediacy of sonic experience and succeeded in bringing the listener close to the very act of composition.[10]

Unlike a number of his works that he acknowledged were prompted by extraneous influences such as occasions (e.g., *Rothko Chapel* to commemorate its opening), honoring friends (*For Philip Guston, For Christian Wolff, For John Cage*), paintings (*The Viola in My Life*) or oriental carpets (*Why Patterns*), *Piano and String Quartet* is a work which seems to have evolved directly and exclusively from Feldman's engagement with sound itself.[11,12]

> [*Piano and String Quartet*] . . . is the history of the speed of the broken chord . . . I mean that's the end and that's the whole piece. I didn't know it

was going to go that way when I wrote it. I thought I'll just trip and something will happen.[13]

Something did happen. Something Steve Reich called "the most beautiful work of [Feldman's] that I know."[14] It was a work that Feldman viewed as a capstone, perhaps a fulfillment of all he had been striving to achieve as a composer: freedom from the bounds of common practice, freedom from the processes and techniques—like serialism—that he viewed as a reaction to and thus an extension of music history and, ultimately and most importantly, the freedom of sound itself.

Piano and String Quartet, arguably Feldman's crowning achievement, is approximately 80 minutes long and, given the date of its composition as well as its duration, falls into the category of his late, longer works. One of the problems that Feldman said he had to address with the longer compositions was "how to keep them going."[15] It is a purpose of this study to examine what it is that keeps *Piano and String Quartet* "going." The analysis in the following chapters will pursue this purpose by describing the overall structure of the composition, its fundamental materials, and the sonic experience of the music itself.

BIOGRAPHICAL BACKGROUND[16]

Morton Feldman was born in New York City on January 12, 1926; his death occurred in 1987. His parents, Irving and Frances, were both émigrés from Russia who had arrived in the United States separately as children: Irving at age 11 in 1901 and Frances at age 3 in 1903. Irving later was employed in the clothing manufacturing business of his elder brother and, by the 1940s, had his own company, making children's coats in Queens, New York.

Feldman's parents recognized his musical talents and started him with piano lessons when he was nine years old at the Third Street Settlement School.[17] Even at this young age, Feldman was composing.[18] At age 12, he began taking piano lessons with Mme. Vera Maurina Press, who knew Alexander Scriabin and had studied with Ferruccio Busoni while living in Germany.

Feldman's aural sensibilities must have been very acute, even as a young person. When he was 14, he told his mother that their piano was no longer adequate. In response, she sent him by himself to the Steinway showroom in Manhattan, where he selected a piano with an "absolutely singular tone."[19] About this piano, Feldman said:

> I still have it, it's "my piano," the others are not pianos. My piano always plays Feldman. If you play Chopin, Schumann, Mozart, on my piano it's always Feldman. . . . The one I have at "Point-point" [a temporary summer residence in France] is very good, but it's not a piano![20]
>
> Somebody once came to my house, and wanted a criticism of their playing—and for some reason played the *Sonatine* by Ravel, and she stopped and she said: "On your piano, it sounds like your music."[21]

In 1941, at age 15, Feldman began composition lessons with Wallingford Riegger. He also began attending the Music and Arts High School in New York City. In April 1943, his first work for string orchestra was performed at the school: *Dirge in Memory of Thomas Wolfe*.[22] In 1944, Feldman began composition lessons with composer Stefan Wolpe, who introduced him to Edgard Varèse. Varèse took an interest in Feldman and—although not formally his student—agreed to meet with him weekly to see his work.

Feldman has credited his becoming a composer to Varèse, stating that Varèse served as a model for "how one could become a professional composer in America, without leading a professional life."[23] Early in his career, he eschewed the idea, not only of earning a living teaching in the halls of the academy—as many composers were doing—but even of attending a university. After graduating from high school, he considered and then rejected the idea of enrolling at New York University. Thus, Feldman did not receive formal university-level academic training in music and composition. Instead, from ages 18 to 41 (i.e., 1944 to 1967), his means of support came from working in his father's coat manufacturing company.[24,25] At the same time, he continued to compose and develop on his own, studying the works of other composers, reading widely, and thinking deeply, especially about aesthetic questions. In 1972, however, he did enter academia as a professor at the State University of New York at Buffalo, and by 1974 had a permanent position as holder of the Edgard Varèse Chair.

Introduction 5

MAJOR INFLUENCES

Feldman's musical and aesthetic trajectory was given shape as a result of a chance encounter with John Cage in late January 1950. Sometime earlier, through Wolpe, he had been introduced to Cage and, recognizing him at a concert at Carnegie Hall in New York (after a performance of Webern's Symphony, op. 21 by the New York Philharmonic, conducted by Dimitri Mitropoulos), struck up a conversation about the music. They became immediate friends, and Feldman soon moved into the apartment building where Cage lived. Cage introduced him to the painters in New York City who were experimenting with new approaches to the visual arts, painters who later became known as abstract expressionists. He became especially close to Philip Guston and Mark Rothko, with whom he shared a common aesthetic vision, but his friendships and influences also included artists such as Jasper Johns, Robert Rauschenberg, and Jackson Pollock, as well as the poet Frank O'Hara. Their cumulative influence was to give metaphorical "permission" for Feldman to follow his natural inclinations as a composer, unafraid to experiment, free to question assumptions and prevailing views about the nature of music, and poised to find the "more direct, more immediate, more physical" sound world that he sought.

> Now, never before was there an aesthetic movement as fresh and new as the abstract painting of the '50s: that complete independence from other art, that complete inner security to work with that which was unknown to them. That was a fantastic aesthetic accomplishment.[26]
>
> [There] was a sort of frontier atmosphere in which an extraordinary *laissez faire* prevailed. . . . This excitement, this social phenomenon, has had an influence extending to much of the painting and music being created today. It reflected a vast permissiveness, tempered with an uncanny instinct for what John Cage would call "the real McCoy."[27]

Eventually, composers Earle Brown and Christian Wolff also became members of this circle of artists and composers around Cage. Feldman, Cage, Brown, and Wolff were like-minded in their searching for new musical sounds and supported each other's creative experiments.

Starting in the late 1970s, Feldman's music was affected by another influence: oriental rugs, of which he had become an avid collector. As with painting, he was a keen observer, always sensitive to the subtlest nuances in color and shape. He translated this observation into what he referred to as "spelling" for string instruments, essentially using double-sharps and double-flats to indicate microtonal adjustments. The first piece in which Feldman used this approach was *Instruments 3*, completed in 1977.

> I would take double sharps and double flats very seriously but not in a Schoenbergian leading-tone way, but it was still related to pitch—but as you know a sharp is a little more directional—and to me it was like adding turpentine to the chromatic field. . . . And if you look at . . . all my recent scores that have string writing . . . I'm very much into the spelling of the strings, not in woodwinds or brass, just the strings. So that's a new concern for me.[28]

> The whole idea of going in tune and out of tune with more precise acoustical instruments [came about in part because of my interest in oriental rugs.] . . . In older oriental rugs the dyes are made in small amounts and so what happens is that there is an imperfection throughout the rug of changing colors of these dyes . . . I interpreted this as going in and out of tune. There is a name for that in rugs—it's called *abrash*—a change of colors that leads us into pieces like *Instruments 3*, which was the beginning of my rug idea.[29]

> [The reason] I use microtonal spelling in the second *Quartet* [Feldman's *String Quartet II* (1983)]—When you're working with a minor 2nd as long as I've been, it gets very wide. I hear a minor 2nd like a minor 3rd almost. . . . But I didn't get the idea conceptually from music at all. I got the idea from—rugs.[30]

Feldman's inspiration from rugs was not limited just to the subtle shifts in colors, but in the case of *Why Patterns?* (1978) came also from the variations in the patterns that make up the rug design.

> *Why Patterns?* is one of the few pieces I ever wrote where I was actually inspired by an extraneous idea, outside of the music itself . . . I had [an oriental] rug that was made up of just a series of borders—the [rugs] I like only have about seven or eight basic colors. There's a variation of the colors, it's called *abrash*. . . . It adds to the rug especially in the refraction of the light on it. And that's what I caught—that the pattern repeats itself, but it's never really exact—It's quite different . . . and the color actually changes because

of—this *abrash*. And I decided to write a piece essentially of patterns, in which [each] one because of the nature of the instrument and the nature of the pattern, is independent, or interdependent from each other.[31]

The instrumentation for *Why Patterns?* is flute/alto flute/bass flute, piano, and glockenspiel. Although these are not the string instruments that were the typical focus of his use of "spelling," Feldman said he chose these instruments because the glockenspiel, "like *abrash*—it's kind of out of tune. And I like the metaphor of going in and out of tune with the various flutes and with the piano."[32]

These influences—Cage, the abstract expressionist painters and paintings, the *abrash* of oriental rugs—were forces throughout Feldman's career, affecting his aesthetic vision generally and inspiring individual works. His experiments with graphic notation are an early example of "the inner security to work with that which was unknown," perhaps Feldman's most fundamental aesthetic aim. The impact of Rauschenberg's photo montages on *The Rothko Chapel* and *The Viola in My Life* written in 1971, and rugs on his late works beginning in 1977, are examples of how extraneous influences inspired specific works.

OVERVIEW OF FELDMAN'S WORKS

Over the course of a career spanning the years 1943 through 1987, Feldman composed approximately 191 works, although he considered compositions written prior to the 1950s as "student" pieces.[33,34] It was not until his association with John Cage in the 1950s that he began to embrace his identity as a composer and thus, in his own mind, the beginning of his "oeuvre." Feldman's works can be divided roughly into three periods: an early period from 1950 to about 1969, a middle period from about 1969 to 1977, and a late period from about 1977 to his death in 1987.

Early Period

In his early period, Feldman focused his efforts toward removing specific choices of pitch, timbre, and time from his compositional procedures. He eventually came to see that standard musical notation, which is designed to specify these elements, was at odds with his purpose. He realized that he needed a different way to present his musical intentions, and so began to experiment with a new graph notation.

His first graph pieces were written in 1950–1953: *Projection 1–5* for soloist and smaller groups and *Intersection 1–4* for orchestra and for soloists.[35,36] These were generally short pieces, with overall durations ranging from 1'30" (*Projection 3*) to 12'30" (*Intersection 1*).

These scores were actually notated on graph paper on which a separate horizontal line was provided for each instrument. Each line contained a series of boxes with squares inside. Each square was assigned a duration; for example, in *Projection 1*, each square had a value of one beat (figure 1.1). Depending on the specific piece, a beat was equal to MM. 72–88. In each box, pitch was not indicated, but rather general indications for register: high, medium, and low. For string instruments, there also were symbols to indicate whether to play arco, pizzicato, and/or with harmonics. Dynamics generally were soft. The decision about what notes to play within the available time was left up to the musicians. This meant that the choice of entrance, to some degree, was also left up to the performers.

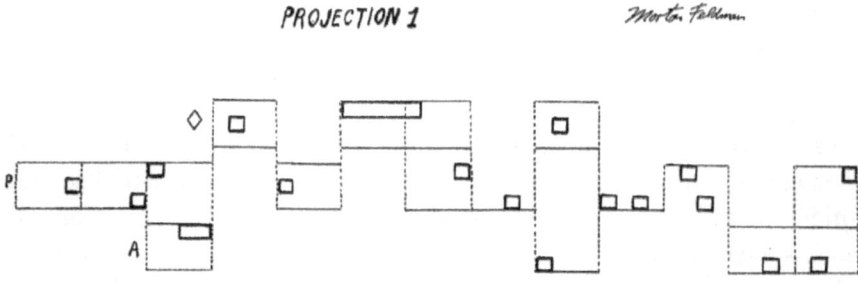

Figure 1.1. Excerpt from Score of Morton Feldman's Projection 1

© Copyright 1961 by C.F. Peters Corporation. Used by permission of C.F. Peters Corporation. All rights reserved.

Always critically self-reflective, Feldman became dissatisfied with the results and began to reconsider his use of graphic notation.

> After several years of writing graph music I began to discover its most serious flaw. I was not only allowing the sounds to be free—I was also liberating the performer. I had never thought of the graph as an art of improvisation, but more as a totally abstract sonic adventure . . . I now understood that if the performers sounded bad it was less because of their lapses of taste than because I was still involved with passages and continuity that allowed their presence to be felt . . . if the means were to be imprecise the result must be terribly clear. And I lacked that sense of clarity to go on.[37]

In the mid-1950s, Feldman turned to precise notation, but at the time found it also to be unsatisfactory for achieving the sound world he sought. He saw it as "too one-dimensional" and without "enough plasticity."[38] He returned to graphic notation again beginning with *Atlantis* (1958) and *Out of Last Pieces* (1960), two works for orchestra. Feldman eventually gave up graphic notation. His last such work, *In Search of an Orchestration*, was written in 1967. Although he had spent nearly 17 years exploring the possibilities of graphic notation, ultimately it did not satisfy his needs in creating the unique sound world he was trying to achieve.

However, during 1960–1961, while still working with graphic notation, Feldman composed a series of works titled *Durations 1–5*, for various combinations of small ensembles.[39] In these works, he experimented with a new notation, using a modified form of standard notation. Pitch, dynamics ("very low"), timbre, and general tempo ("slow") are specified, but duration is not. The musicians begin at the same time, and then are free to choose the durations of the notes that Feldman provided (figure 1.2).

Middle Period

Beginning around 1969, Feldman turned to precise notation almost exclusively, specifying pitch, timbre, meter, dynamics, and duration. Between 1969 and 1977, he composed 41 works. These include *On Time and the Instrumental Factor* (1969), *The Viola in My Life 1–4* (1970–1971), *Rothko Chapel* (1972), *For Frank O'Hara* (1973), *Instruments 1–2* (1974–1975), *Neither*, a one-act opera for soprano and orchestra on a libretto by Samuel Beckett (1977), and *Instruments 3* (1977).

Figure 1.2. Excerpt from Score of Morton Feldman's Durations 1
© Copyright 1962 by C.F. Peters Corporation. Used by permission of C.F. Peters Corporation. All rights reserved.

During this period, Feldman continued to employ small ensembles with a wide range of instrumentation, as well as writing some pieces for orchestra. Instrumentation itself became his primary source of inspiration.

> For me composition is orchestration, and so what leads me to begin a composition is a weight, an orchestration which is new for me.[40]

Virtually all of the compositions of this period are in one movement.

> Form as I know it no longer exists. . . . And to me form . . . is only the separation of things into parts. Not the relationship in the separation of things into parts, but just separating things. First movement, second movement, slow movement.[41]

Late Period: Longer Works

During his middle period, Feldman's compositions tended to be 25–35 minutes in length. Toward the end of the 1970s, he began to question the penchant for pieces of this duration. He realized that many of his pieces, those of his contemporaries (e.g., Elliott Carter, Steve Reich, and Ralph Shapey), and even many orchestral masterpieces (e.g., Stravinsky's *Rite of Spring* and Bartók's *Music for Strings, Percussion and Celesta*) were about 25–35 minutes in length. This prompted him to ask himself: "What would I write if I just didn't think about the length—what would I write if I didn't think about the audience?"[42]

Feldman addressed this question of longer works beginning in 1979, first with *Violin and Orchestra*, about 52 minutes in length, and then *String Quartet*, his first truly long work, of approximately 94 minutes duration. His last work—*Piano, Violin, Viola, Cello*—written in 1987, the year of his death, ran about 75 minutes. During this period of 1979–1987, he wrote 27 compositions, of which 13 could be considered longer works. These longer works have durations ranging from about 75 minutes (*For John Cage*) to 5½ hours (*String Quartet II*).

In writing these longer compositions, Feldman, as always, was questioning assumptions and breaking down barriers.

> It's the option of writing very long pieces that are very difficult to play, very difficult to hear and have to do with the life of the piece, whatever that means, and not the life of the performer, or what happens to an audience when they go hear it. I'm trying to see what happens when the work does not depend on those other very important, very rigid factors.[43]

Among these assumptions and barriers, the nature of form was a central concern.

> For me, the focus (not discounting my material) was more on what happens to the form of the music as the length of an ostensibly "one movement" work is extended beyond what was familiar to me. . . . What developed in *String Quartet* might be best described as a "novel" form, where one's sense of time is somewhat more displaced than in a musical composition, and where chronological information aids our insight in understanding the "story," rather than the cause-and-effect syndrome which is so indigenous to how we listen to music.[44]

> Form is a control restricted to a certain lifestyle that somebody doesn't question. . . . The ending of *Crippled Symmetry* could never have happened in a twenty-minute piece. . . . That's not form, that's scale.[45]

Feldman composed *Piano and String Quartet* during this period, and with a duration of about 80 minutes, it is one of the late long works.

Feldman's compositions often were written with specific musicians in mind, and *Piano and String Quartet* is a particular case in point. The autograph score has the inscription "for Aki Takahashi and the Kronos Quartet," with whom he had had a long musical friendship. They premiered it on November 2, 1985, and recorded it during November 1991.[46]

The Kronos Quartet had premiered *String Quartet* and *String Quartet II*. But the playing of pianist Aki Takahashi was evidently an element of particular importance to Feldman as he worked on *Piano and String Quartet*.

> In Aki's quintet—and it is Aki's quintet, I wouldn't have written it without Aki.[47]

> When I'm writing for an instrumental combination and especially for someone who I am writing for, I think about how they project. They're not just playing notes, it's this person playing. The *Piano and String Quartet* could not have been written without the way Aki plays and also her concentration, which is transmitted. She just doesn't look concentrated—with Aki, it's like a séance, it's transmitted.[48]

Piano and String Quartet was completed on September 20, 1985. It is not known when Feldman began this piece. However, there is evidence that Aki Takahashi knew that he was working on it earlier in 1985. She wrote to him on August 23, 1985, asking "And how is the piece for piano and string quartet going? I really can't wait."[49] Feldman replied on September 11, saying, "Never expected to write a piece with just broken chords!"[50]

In fact, *Piano and String Quartet* may be considered a study in the various forms that broken chords can take. On July 6, 1986, during the aforementioned lecturing at Middelburg, Holland, Feldman said, "[*Piano and String Quartet*] is the history of the speed of the broken chord—and it became very funny: four notes, three notes, two notes—what's a broken one note? Just a little grace note before it."[51] As the analysis that follows in the next chapters will show, the conception of "broken chords," understood expansively, pervades the piece and takes many forms.

OVERVIEW OF PUBLISHED ANALYSES OF FELDMAN'S WORKS

Despite the fact that Feldman's iconoclastic music presents unique challenges to analysis, a good number of analysts have risen to the challenge.

Analyses of more than 40 of his almost 200 compositions have been published in several languages in books and juried journals in the United States, Europe, Russia, and South America. A selected listing of this published work can be found in appendix C.

More than half (24) of these analyses examine compositions from Feldman's early period. In addition, analyses of five works from the middle period and 14 from the late period have been published. Some individual works have been analyzed by more than one analyst. Of the 14 late period works, there are 10 analyses in English, which will be discussed below (NB, the citations for each of the analyses are in appendix C). However, none of these analyses of late-period works have addressed *Piano and String Quartet*.

Five studies of his late works address the entire composition, building from local details to argue for the presence of a large-scale structure. Terrence Paynter, examining patterns of pitch, register, and rhythm in *Spring of Chosroes* (1977), identified a formal ABA' structure, with parallelisms in section B suggesting a palindrome. In her study of *Piano* (1977), Paula Ames argues that the piece has three sections (A, B, C) and a coda. She supports her view by showing how each section contrasts in terms of melodic/harmonic pattern, texture, dynamics, and register. In a section separate from the analysis, Ames also addresses a range of matters concerning performance practice related to *Piano* (e.g., pacing, articulation, and pedaling). Steven Johnson examines *Why Patterns?* (1978) in its entirety, but does not propose an overarching structure. Instead, he diagrams the patterned pitch and harmonic segments assigned uniquely to each of the three instruments (flute, piano, and glockenspiel), and compares the sonic experience of *Why Patterns?* to the art and aesthetics of Jasper Johns.

Feldman's *Triadic Memories* (1981) is examined by Johnson and Edward Jurkowski in separate essays. Both analyze the complete work, but use different methods. Jurkowski focuses on changes in texture as the primary criterion for identifying the structure of the work. He suggests that the large-scale structure of *Triadic Memories* is comprised of five major parts and a coda. Johnson takes a wholly different approach. As he did with his analysis of *Why Patterns?*, Johnson compares *Triadic Memories* to the aesthetics of another artist and his work—in this case, Samuel Beckett and his novel *Molloy* (1947). Citing the "aimlessness, uncertainty, disintegration, and paralysis" that characterize Beckett's writing, Johnson charts a timeline of the main motifs comprised in *Triadic Memories* and discusses how their appearance and disappearance illustrate these same characteristics.

Wes York's analysis of *For John Cage* (1982) examines pitch, instrumentation, register, and rhythm at the local level and finds nested variations of symmetrical structures, basically ABA in form locally and large-scale. He identifies five sections to the piece, the component subsections of each section, and, within subsections, groupings of phrases based on the intervals formed by the pitch material.

The remaining five analyses do not claim to provide a synthesis of the overarching or large-scale structure of the work at hand, but offer instead an examination of specific sections or fundamental musical elements. Christian Wolff's somewhat detailed liner notes for the Flux Quartet recording of *String Quartet II* is an example of the latter. In what he calls a "provisional" analysis, Wolff describes a set of key distinctive patterns that comprise the work. These patterns include the semitone pitch structure of the opening gesture, the five dynamic levels that are used, and textural changes (e.g., broken chords, three-instrument chords followed by a single instrument, four-instrument chords played chorale-like, and solo cello playing oscillating whole-note figures).

In three different published works, Dora Hanninen discusses four of Feldman's late compositions. In an article in which she sets forth her theory of recontextualization in music, Hanninen (2003) examines the repetition of patterns exemplified in a short passage from *Crippled Symmetry* (1983), using it as a framework for presenting her concept of recontextualization. Through separate detailed case studies of selected passages from *Coptic Light* (1985) and *Piano, Violin, Viola, Cello* (1987), Hanninen (2004) presents methods for experiencing and analyzing the composer's late works in terms of his use of scale (presented in the article as Case Study I, on *Coptic Light*) and repetition (Case Study II, on *Piano, Violin, Viola, Cello*). In her comprehensive theoretical treatise on musical analysis, Hanninen (2012) devotes a chapter to *Palais de Mari* (1986), analyzing the opening (mm. 1–73) and closing (mm. 287–437) passages in detail. She notes the difficulty of ascertaining form in through-composed pieces such as *Palais de Mari* (and by extension, most of Feldman's works), and proposes that analysts consider the approach set forth in the chapter to address such difficulties.

There are several important conclusions to draw from this survey of the analytical work on Feldman's compositions. First, competent analysis of his works is possible, whether from the early, middle, or late periods. Second, there are a variety of methods and approaches that can be used to analyze his compositions. And finally, works from the late period are amenable to descriptions of large-scale or overall structure. These conclusions guide the analysis of *Piano and String Quartet*, the work that is the subject of this study.

NOTES

1. Feldman, Morton, ed. Raoul Mörchen, *Morton Feldman in Middelburg: Words on Music—Lectures and Conversations, Vol. 1* (Köln: Ed. MusikTexte, 2008), 464.
2. "Walter Zimmerman Conversation with Morton Feldman, November 1975," in Chris Villars, *Morton Feldman Says* (London: Hyphen Press, 2006), 52.
3. "Darmstadt Lecture, July 1984," in Villars, 208.
4. Gagne, C., and Caras, T., "Morton Feldman [interview]," in *Soundpieces: Interviews with American Composers* (Metuchen, NJ: Scarecrow Press, 1982), 170.
5. Feldman, Morton, *Morton Feldman in Middelburg*, 464.
6. Feldman, Morton, ed. B. H. Friedman, *Give My Regards to Eighth Street* (Cambridge: Exact Exchange, 2002), 27–28.
7. Ibid., 26.
8. "Toronto Lecture, April 1982," in Villars, 146.
9. Feldman, Morton, Liner notes, "Feldman, Brown," Time Records No. 58007, 1963, New York.
10. DeLio, Thomas, in DeLio, Thomas, ed., *The Music of Morton Feldman* (Westport, CT: Greenwood Press, 1996), xiv.
11. Gagne, C., and Caras, T., "Morton Feldman [interview]," in *Soundpieces: Interviews with American Composers* (Metuchen, NJ: Scarecrow Press, 1982), 170.
12. "Johannesburg Lecture, 2 August 1983," in Villars, 178.
13. Feldman, Morton, *Morton Feldman in Middelburg*, 466.
14. Reich, Steve, *Writings on Music* (Oxford; New York: Oxford University Press, 2002), 57.
15. Feldman, Morton, *Morton Feldman in Middelburg*, 94, 124, 198, 604 (*Vol. 2*).

16. The biographical information in this section is based on Sebastien Claren's "A Feldman Chronology," translated by Christine Shuttleworth, in Villars, 255–58.

17. Founded in 1894 as a social service agency for immigrants, it was part of the 19th-century settlement house movement in the United States, but specialized in providing music lessons. Today it is known as the Third Street Music School, located on the Lower East Side of Manhattan.

18. Feldman, Morton, *Give My Regards to Eighth Street*, 112.

19. Claren, Sebastien, "A Feldman Chronology," translated by Christine Shuttleworth, in Villars, 256.

20. Cadieu, Martine, "Morton Feldman—Waiting," in Villars, 39. "Point-point" was Feldman's mispronunciation of Pontpont, the French village where he was housed to work on *Rothko Chapel* by the patrons who had commissioned the work, John and Dominique de Menil.

21. "Kevin Volans Conversation with Morton Feldman, 26 July 1984," in Villars, 215.

22. High School of Music and the Arts Concert Program, found at microfilm page 207, 1-0536, held in the Morton Feldman Archive at the Paul Sacher Stiftung, Basel, Switzerland.

23. Claren, Sebastien, "A Feldman Chronology," translated by Christine Shuttleworth, in Villars, 257.

24. Feldman, Morton, *Give My Regards to Eighth Street*, 112.

25. Thus, Feldman's quote about being "like a tailor" is both truthful and an example of his playfulness and penchant for inside jokes, characteristics present in his music as well.

26. "Robert Ashley Interview, August 1984," in Villars, 15–16.

27. Feldman, Morton, *Give My Regards to Eighth Street*, 15.

28. "Toronto Lecture, April 1982," in Villars, 144.

29. "Jan Williams Interview, 22 April 1983," in Villars, 155.

30. "Darmstadt Lecture, July 1984," in Villars, 198.

31. "Johannesburg Lecture, 2 August 1983," in Villars, 178.

32. Ibid., 178.

33. Feldman, Morton, "List of Works," in *Morton Feldman in Middelburg: Words on Music—Lectures and Conversations, Vol. 2,* ed. Raoul Mörchen (Köln: Ed. MusikTexte, 2008), 876–82.

34. "Jan Williams Interview, 22 April 1983," in Villars, 151.

35. *Projection 1* (cello solo, 1950), *Projection 2* (flute, trumpet, violin, cello, and piano, 1951), *Projection 3* (two pianos, 1951), *Projection 4* (violin and piano, 1951), *Projection 5* (three flutes, trumpet, three cellos, and two pianos, 1951).

36. *Intersection 1* (orchestra, 1951), *Marginal Intersection* (orchestra, 1951), *Intersection 2* (piano solo, 1951), *Intersection 3* (piano solo, 1951), *Intersection 4* (cello solo, 1953).

37. Feldman, Morton, *Give My Regards to Eighth Street*, 6.

38. Ibid.

39. *Durations 1* (alto flute, piano, violin, cello, 1960), *Durations 2* (cello, and piano, 1960), *Durations 3* (violin, tuba, pianos, 1961), *Durations 4* (vibraphone, violin, cello, 1961), *Durations 5* (horn, vibraphone, harp, piano/celesta, cello, 1961).

40. "Morton Feldman Talks to Paul Griffiths, August 1972," in Villars, 48.

41. Feldman, Morton, *Morton Feldman in Middelburg*, 148–50.

42. "Toronto Lecture, 1982," in Villars, 139. Feldman also credited the impetus for his long works to "*The Art of Memory*" by Frances Yates. He said, "I was very impressed with the book, and it was the beginning of my long pieces. I think, without the book there wouldn't have been the long pieces." Feldman, Morton, *Morton Feldman in Middelburg*, 472–76.

43. "Peter Gena Interview, 1982," in Villars, 131.

44. "String Quartet," in Feldman, Morton, *Give My Regards to Eighth Street*, 133.

45. Feldman, Morton, *Morton Feldman in Middelburg*, 152.

46. The premiere performance was at the New Music America "85" concert in the Bing Theater at the Los Angeles County Museum of Art.

47. Feldman, Morton, *Morton Feldman in Middelburg*, 466.

48. Ibid., 470.

49. Letter to Morton Feldman from Aki Takashi found at microfilm page 207, 1-781, held in the Morton Feldman Archive at the Paul Sacher Stiftung, Basel, Switzerland.

50. Aki Takahashi shared a photocopy of a partial page of the letter with the author; see appendix B.

51. Feldman, Morton, *Morton Feldman in Middelburg*, 466.

Chapter Two

Analytical Approach

OVERVIEW

The score used for this analysis is a copy of Morton Feldman's autograph, completed and signed by the composer on September 20, 1985, and published by Universal Edition.[1] The score has three systems per page, with nine measures in every system. Although the score has page numbers, there are no measure numbers, rehearsal marks, or any other mechanism for identifying specific places in the score.

Accordingly, the examples used throughout this discussion, as well as annotations such as measure numbers, were prepared by the author. Some measures or groups of measures are to be repeated. These are indicated in the score by repeat signs or by multiple repeats (e.g., "3×'s," "5×'s," etc.) written above a measure with repeat signs. For the sake of simplicity and clarity, each measure has been numbered in sequence, regardless of the number of times the measure is to be repeated. However, repetitions have been considered in calculating the durations of musical material.[2]

Although Feldman claimed to eschew "sectionalizing" his music, and that his aesthetic was rooted in "the sound" more than any other factor, it is apparent that there are separable areas of activity in *Piano and String Quartet*.[3,4] For the purpose of discussion, these areas will be labeled parts and sections, though they are in no way comparable to the formal notion of parts and sections in a more traditional conception of form. Specifically, in Feldman's work the material in each part or section is only discernable as unified as that part or section evolves. In other words, there are no clear markers delineating beginnings and endings as there are with traditional cadential designs. As will be shown, however, the separable areas of activity of *Piano and String Quartet* comprise a clear, purposeful structure. This structure consists of three major parts. Within each part, there are several sections, and within each section there may be subsections. These will be described in detail in the following chapters.

As noted in the introduction, "the sound" of a Feldman work begins with its "orchestration," that is, the choice of instruments. This is especially true of *Piano and String Quartet,* and the ways in which the salient distinctions in sonic characteristics between the two types of instruments are exploited. Therefore, a brief discussion of these sonic characteristics is in order.

Sounds in the violin, viola, cello (i.e., "the strings"), and piano are produced through the vibration of strings. This makes their sound production and timbre unlike that of the wind instruments, idiophones, and membranophones. In the piano, the vibration is set in motion by hammers striking the strings, which produce attack noise and, when the damper pedal is down, an extended sustain and decay. Vibration in the string instruments is initiated with the bow or by using the fingers to pluck the strings. The bow controls attack noise (depending on the strength of the attack and, relatedly, dynamics) and the length of sustain; with the release of the bow, there is virtually no decay. When plucking the strings, the length of sustain is controlled by dampening; when not dampened, there can be a minimal experience of decay.

Feldman capitalizes on these similarities and differences in *Piano and String Quartet.* In fact, the manipulation and comparison/contrast of attack, sustain, and decay in these instruments—whether in concordance or opposition—is an important feature of this work.[5] The dynamics are pianississimo throughout the work for all of the instruments and the strings are muted. Thus, the piano has minimal, but noticeable, attack noise and the strings have virtually none, except in the few pizzicato passages. For the piano, the damper pedal is down for the complete work. Thus, decay in the piano and its absence in the strings, as well as differences in attack noise (somewhat noticeable when the strings are bowed), are played off against one another and serve a prominent role throughout the piece.

The score has no tempo marking. Therefore, one must look for guidance from the recording of *Piano and String Quartet* by Aki Takahashi and the Kronos Quartet (who premiered the work under Feldman's supervision) as well as general knowledge of Feldman's style.[6] With a total duration of 8,814.5 eighth notes in the composition, and the recording length of approximately 79.5 minutes, the tempo as actually performed is calculated to be quarter note = MM. 55.4.[7]

The unchanging, very slow tempo and very soft dynamics, together with the multiple repetitions of musical elements throughout the work, as well as its very long total duration, create an aural experience that on the surface seems very static to the listener. As such, its moment-to-moment character is without apparent dramatic change. However, this flat surface belies a great deal of microcosmic change of activity that results in widely varying degrees of stasis and instability over the course of the composition. This activity is very subtle and its effect is typically perceived subconsciously, with awareness requiring close attention to sonic details.

Perhaps it is best described as the difference between looking directly at a sample of pond water and seeing the teeming life held within under a microscope. The tension in this opposition of static surface at the macro level and sub-surface activity at the micro level is central to the experience of this composition. It is essential to keep this macro/micro opposition in mind as a continuing backdrop to the analysis. This is because, whether cognitively perceived or unconsciously sensed, the purposeful exploitation of stasis and instability that arises from this opposition is at the heart of the structure through which *Piano and String Quartet* evolves.

CRITERIA AND PROCEDURES

One aim of this analysis is to describe the large-scale structure of *Piano and String Quartet*, including its major parts and sections. To discern the structure of the composition, three criteria were used: musical texture, pitch and harmonic content, and the foregrounding of either the piano or the string instruments.[8] These criteria, taken together, cross-validate assertions made about the structure. Before proceeding with the analysis of the composition, these three criteria will be explained in detail.

TEXTURE

Texture is a defining characteristic that demarcates the three-part large-scale structure of *Piano and String Quartet*. Each of these three parts is marked by an internally consistent, distinct, and recognizable type of texture, or set of textures. Indeed, these internally consistent textures undergird the sonic character of the respective parts. However, the change to a new texture—defining the start of a new structural division—is foreshadowed in the section that precedes it.

There are several general characteristics that distinguish the types of texture in *Piano and String Quartet*. These include:

- The number of instruments playing at any time
- Whether the piano or the strings are in the foreground
- The number of tones sounded simultaneously
- The kinds of interaction among the instruments, especially between piano and strings
- Articulation

A typology of textures specific to *Piano and String Quartet* was derived inductively from examining the score. Initially, and most obviously, one may note three main textural distinctions: piano playing alone, piano and strings playing together, and strings playing alone. What is most important is that Feldman's use of these textures brings the listener's attention to the relationship between the piano and the strings. This, in turn, helps the listener recognize the different regions of activity in the composition that are the basis of its structure.

Piano Alone

The texture type labeled Piano Alone occurs in two different forms: the piano plays either single notes or broken chords, without string accompaniment. The form using single notes has a very easily recognizable quality, being limited to a few specific pitch classes (e.g., C, D♭, D, E♭) and often characterized by large leaps upward and downward.[9] These can be considered as intervallic cells and are varied by manipulation of rhythm and meter, pitch, inversion, register, and transposition (figure 2.1).[10] This first form will be labeled as the texture type Piano Alone/Single Notes.

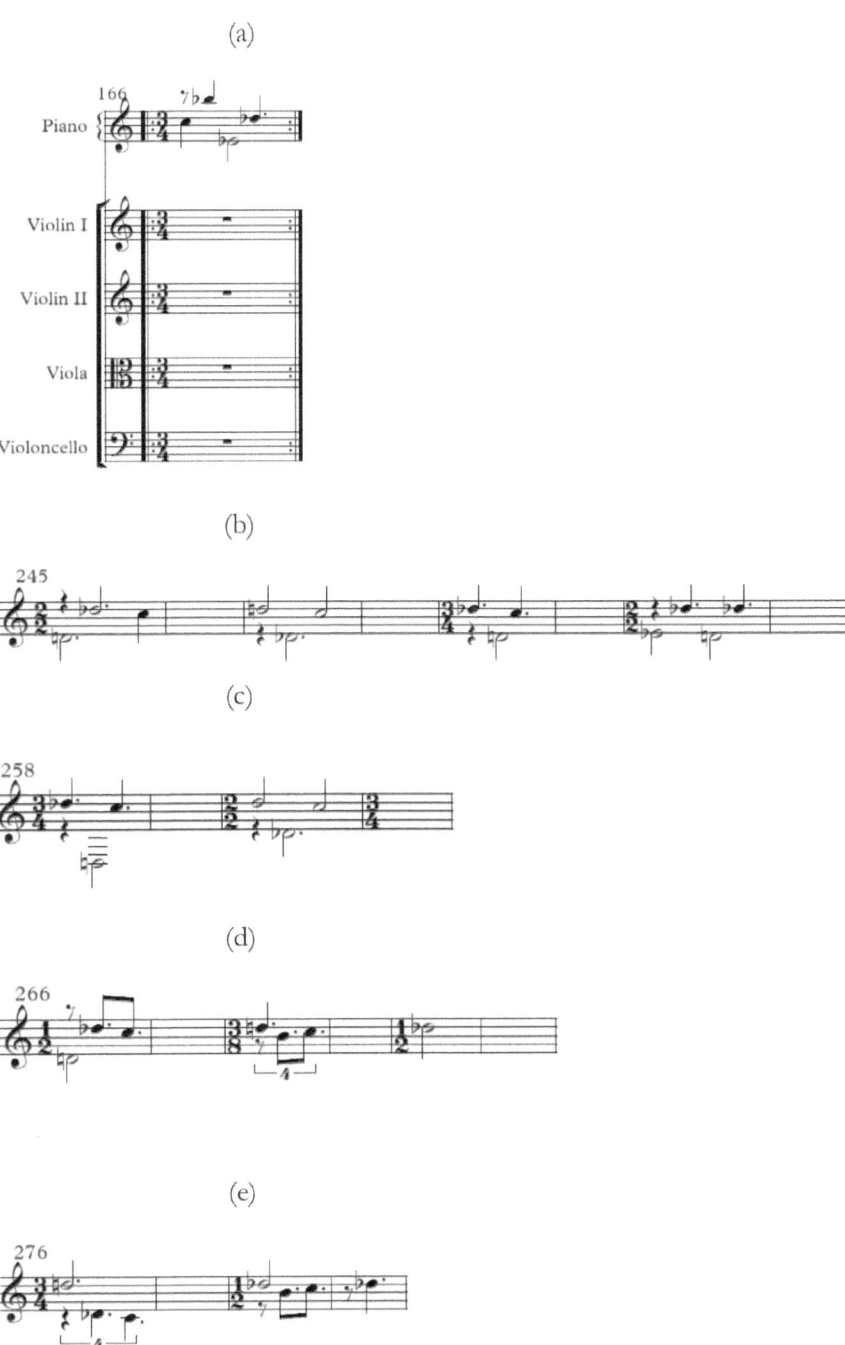

Figure 2.1. Morton Feldman *Piano and String Quartet*
© Copyright 1985 by Universal Edition (London) Ltd., London / UE17972

The second form of this texture type is labeled Piano Alone/Broken Chords. It appears in two versions: as a single chord and as pairs of chords. When appearing as a single chord, "brokenness" takes three guises: completely rolled, partially rolled, and with a grace note followed by a single sounding of the remaining notes in the chord—Feldman's "broken one note" (figure 2.2).[11]

Figure 2.2. Morton Feldman *Piano and String Quartet*
© Copyright 1985 by Universal Edition (London) Ltd., London / UE17972

When appearing in pairs, each chord is always completely rolled (figure 2.3).

Figure 2.3. Morton Feldman *Piano and String Quartet*
© Copyright 1985 by Universal Edition (London) Ltd., London / UE17972

Piano and Strings

The texture type Piano and Strings has three main categories, each with its respective variants. The three main categories are here labeled Simultaneous, Antiphonal, and Dovetail. In the Simultaneous category, the piano and strings are sounded at the same time. In the Antiphonal category, the piano and the strings alternate soundings. Dovetail is characterized by overlapping soundings of the piano and strings.

Simultaneous

The fundamental characteristic of the Piano and Strings/Simultaneous texture category is that the sounding of piano and strings occurs at the same time and is sustained for the same note value, regardless of the duration of the piano decay. There are several variants of this texture type, which include the piano playing a single note and all four strings playing a tetrachord; the piano playing a hexachord and the strings playing a dyad, trichord, or tetrachord; and the piano playing a hexachord with a single note in the strings (figure 2.4).

Figure 2.4. Morton Feldman *Piano and String Quartet*
© Copyright 1985 by Universal Edition (London) Ltd., London / UE17972

26   Chapter Two

Antiphonal

In the Antiphonal texture category, musical material in the piano may be answered by musical material in the strings, or vice versa. Despite local variants, a "call and response" type of alternating pattern is common to all passages within this category. Such local variants may consist of a single note gesture in the piano answered by a tetrachord in the strings, a broken chord in the piano alternating with a single note in the strings, a broken chord in the piano alternating with a tetrachord in the strings (either broken or not), or a simultaneous sounding in the piano and strings alternating with a broken chord in the piano (figure 2.5).

Figure 2.5. Morton Feldman *Piano and String Quartet*
© Copyright 1985 by Universal Edition (London) Ltd., London / UE17972

Dovetail

The distinguishing characteristic of the Dovetail texture category is the overlap of soundings between the piano and the strings. Feldman varies the basic Dovetail texture in a number of ways. These include a broken piano chord overlapping with a string tetrachord that is not broken, overlapping broken chords in both piano and strings, and a single note in the piano overlapping with a tetrachord in the strings (figure 2.6). The examples show that this texture is executed in slightly different ways, but always with clearly overlapping soundings between piano and strings.

Figure 2.6. Morton Feldman *Piano and String Quartet*
© Copyright 1985 by Universal Edition (London) Ltd., London / UE17972

28   Chapter Two

One may wonder how the back and forth of soundings in the Dovetail texture differs from the "call and response" type of texture of Antiphonal, especially given the long decay of the piano in the latter. What sets the two apart, in my view, is the proximity of sounding to release. Antiphonal figure 2.5(d) shows unambiguously that the piano sounding in measure 436 does not begin until after the release of the strings in measure 435. This represents a clear difference with Dovetail figure 2.6(a), in which the first piano sounding/sustain bridges the first sounding and release of the strings to the second sounding of the strings.

Although distinct as a texture, Dovetail could be considered Antiphonal in diminution. As with the potentially expansive definition of "brokenness," this kind of extension/transformation of musical material certainly would be among Feldman's compositional inclinations. For this analysis, the sonic experience of a texture will be a factor in deeming it Antiphonal or Dovetail.

Strings Alone

The texture type Strings Alone appears in three forms: broken tetrachords, tetrachord pairs, and single notes.

Broken Tetrachords

Feldman creates broken tetrachords in the strings by overlapping the sequence of sounding and/or release of the notes played by the four instruments (figure 2.7). Sonically, this texture is an echo, or quasi-simulation, of the sounding and decay of the fully rolled broken chord in the piano (e.g., see the piano part, figure 2.4(b), mm. 3–8).

Figure 2.7.   Morton Feldman *Piano and String Quartet*
© Copyright 1985 by Universal Edition (London) Ltd., London / UE17972

Tetrachord Pairs

The texture Strings Alone/Tetrachord Pairs consists of two different tetrachords that are repeated. The repetitions may be varied rhythmically, occur identically, or be executed multiple times (figure 2.8).

Figure 2.8.   Morton Feldman *Piano and String Quartet*
© Copyright 1985 by Universal Edition (London) Ltd., London / UE17972

Single Notes

The texture Strings Alone/Single Notes is unique within this composition and played only by the cello (figure 2.9). Comprised of 14 or 15 notes extended over five measures, it is the only instance of a long single-note

Figure 2.9.   Morton Feldman *Piano and String Quartet*
© Copyright 1985 by Universal Edition (London) Ltd., London / UE17972

gesture in *Piano and String Quartet*. This gesture appears five times in varied forms, starting, respectively, in measures 210, 226, 289, 451, and 490. As it is so unique within the piece, this gesture serves as a distinct marker in the composition.

SUMMARY

The preceding discussion has set forth a description of categories of texture employed by Feldman in *Piano and String Quartet*. The three main categories are Piano Alone, Piano and Strings, and Strings Alone. Within each of these categories are multiple variants. These categories are intended to be exhaustive and mutually exclusive.

However, it is essential to recognize the limits of any strict definition when confronting the degree of variance and manipulation wrought by Feldman's musical inventiveness and playfulness. For example, where a more expansive definition would have changed the category for a particular variant, this was addressed above (for instance, whether the piano intervallic cell should be considered as single notes or as a broken chord). Another example has to do with the forms that brokenness takes in the strings. Although brokenness in the strings appears in only one form in the Strings Alone texture (i.e., figure 2.7), it appears in additional forms in other textures. In figure 2.5(c) the sounding of the strings is "broken" but the release is simultaneous. In figure 2.6(b), brokenness is executed through overlapping soundings in pairs of string instruments. While it is important to recognize these subtle differences, it should be kept in mind that they are local in their effect. As will become apparent, interpreting them one way or the other would not change the large-scale structure of *Piano and String Quartet*.

PITCH AND HARMONIC CONTENT

The second major criterion for identifying regions of activity in the piece (i.e., parts, sections, and subsections) is the pitch and harmonic content of *Piano and String Quartet*. Although Feldman is neither a serialist nor a creator of interconnected pitch-class sets (as identified by Allen Forte), he does use all 12 tones throughout this atonal composition. It is important to stress that in discussing pitch design in this piece, one makes a distinction between formal structures in which pitch is used to create a progressive evolution of sonic relationships and formal structures in which pitch and intervals are used as recognizable entities (or "colors") which recur and may be varied for their sound, but do not evolve.[12] *Piano and String Quartet* is an example of the latter.

To analyze the pitch and harmonic content, two procedures were followed. First, pitch classes were assigned the numbers 0–11 to represent each of the 12 sequential chromatic pitch classes from C-B. To exemplify this approach, figure 2.10 displays the notes in the cello gesture in figure 2.9 with numbered pitch classes added below the staff.

Figure 2.10. Morton Feldman *Piano and String Quartet*
© Copyright 1985 by Universal Edition (London) Ltd., London / UE17972

Second, this numbering system was expanded to analyze and describe the chords that appear in the composition. The analysis began with assigning each note of the chord its pitch-class number, ordering the numbers to ensure the smallest interval of the outer terms, determining the size of each successive interval in the sequence, and naming the chord according to the size of each successive interval. For example, the piano chord in measure 1 is comprised of the pitches D♯(3), B♭(10), E(4), G(7), F♯(6), and A♭(8) (figure 2.11). These were reordered as pitch classes 3, 4, 6, 7, 8, 10. The size of the interval between pitch class "3" and "4" is 1, between "4" and "6" is 2, and so forth, resulting in identifying it as a 1-2-1-1-2 hexachord. Using this approach, all inversions, variants, or transpositions of this hexachord will be identified as 1-2-1-1-2.

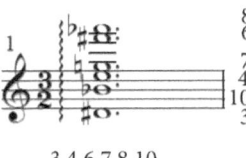

Figure 2.11. Morton Feldman *Piano and String Quartet*
© Copyright 1985 by Universal Edition (London) Ltd., London / UE17972

3,4,6,7,8,10
1-2-1-1-2

32 Chapter Two

FOREGROUND/BACKGROUND

Not surprisingly, whether the piano or strings is in the foreground is a form-defining element in *Piano and String Quartet*. Determining what is foreground is based upon a number of factors considered simultaneously. The first is the comparative duration of the presence of the piano versus the strings. The second is the use of repetition of a chord or gesture. The third is the amount of activity in a repeated chord or gesture.

The first 10 measures of *Piano and String Quartet* will serve as illustration (figure 2.12). The damper pedal is down during all of the composition. This means that the sounding of the piano is heard in measures 1, 3, 5, 7, and 9, with the decay of the piano being heard in measures 2, 4, 6, 8, and 10. In contrast, the strings are heard only in measures 1, 3, 5, 7, and 9. Thus, the piano has greater duration than the strings in these measures. The piano chord is repeated in the same way five times and, although there is some repetition in the strings, there is more activity in the brokenness of the completely rolled piano hexachord. The sonic experience of the piano in the foreground is thus supported by—or a result of—these quantitative factors.

Figure 2.12. Morton Feldman *Piano and String Quartet*
© Copyright 1985 by Universal Edition (London) Ltd., London / UE17972

SUMMARY AND CONCLUSION

The three criteria described above—texture, pitch and harmonic content, and foreground/background emphasis—will be the basis for determining the structure of *Piano and String Quartet*. Each of these criteria has several components and/or variants. They have been described in detail to explain the analytical approach taken and to serve as the predicate for the presentation of the structure of *Piano and String Quartet* in the chapters that follow.

NOTES

1. Morton Feldman, *Piano and String Quartet* © Copyright 1985 by Universal Edition (London) Ltd., London/UE 17972.
2. Appendix A provides a key for locating measure numbers in the autograph score that are referenced in the analysis.
3. "Toronto Lecture, April 1982," in Chris Villars, *Morton Feldman Says* (London: Hyphen Press, 2006), 139.
4. Feldman, Morton, *Morton Feldman: Essays*, ed. Walter Zimmerman (Kerpen, West Germany: Beginner Press, 1985), 38.
5. Feldman explained why he was so focused on attack and decay in his composing: "Change [i.e., variation] is the only solution to an unchanging aural plane created by the constant element of projection, of attack. This is perhaps why in my own music I am so involved with the decay of each sound, and try to make its attack sourceless. The attack of a sound is not its character. Actually what we hear is the attack and not the sound. Decay, however, this departing landscape, *this* expresses where the sound exists in our hearing—leaving us rather than coming toward us." Feldman, Morton, "The Anxiety of Art," in *Give My Regards to Eighth Street*, ed. B. H. Friedman (Cambridge, MA: Exact Change, 2000), 25.
6. Kronos Quartet and Aki Takahashi, *Piano and String Quartet* (recording), New York: Elektra Nonesuch 979320-2, 1991/1993. Nonesuch has provided this recording to YouTube on the Kronos Channel at https://www.youtube.com/results?search_query=kronos+piano+and+string+quartet.
7. It is not unusual for the tempo of Feldman's late works to be slow. The tempo marking for his composition *Piano* (1981) is quarter note = *circa* 63; for *Palais de Mari for Piano* (1986) the tempo marking is quarter note = 63–66. A tempo marking is absent from the score for *Triadic Memories* (1987), but appears to be very slow from the recording by Aki Takahashi. Assumptions about

the tempo of *Piano and String Quartet* take this into account, as well as personal communications with two of the performers who premiered and recorded the work, and knew Feldman well. David Harrington of the Kronos Quartet, in a personal communication with the author on March 28, 2017, stated that there are no notes from the composer appended to the performer scores that were used in the rehearsal with Feldman for the premiere of *Piano and String Quartet* and for the recording. He said that the performance on the recording was consistent with how it was played during the rehearsal with Feldman and at the premiere, which Feldman approved (see appendix D for the interview with Harrington). Aki Takahashi also confirmed, in a personal communication on May 22, 2018, that there are no tempo markings on her score. Thus the recording of *Piano and String Quartet* stands as the only extant, although indirect, source for assertions about the intended tempo of the composition.

8. The terms "harmonic" and "harmonically" as used herein refer to the pitch and interval material as constructed by Feldman for *Piano and String Quartet*; no application of classical harmonic theory is intended nor should be inferred.

9. Even though the character of the single note gestures in figure 2.1 is very clear as such and recognizable sonically, it is also possible to think of them as broken tetrachords or trichords, given the durational overlap of pitches and the fact that the damper pedal is down. However, for the purposes of this analysis, the definition of "broken chord" will not be expanded that far.

10. For example, the switch to pitch classes B, C, D♭, and D in figure 2.1 is a T11 transposition.

11. The use of the term "sounded" or "sounding" rather than "attack" is being used because Feldman intended the sounds to be as attackless as possible (see note 5).

12. Feldman's brief 1984 essay on *String Quartet II* (1984) contrasts "constructing a 'composition'" and "assemblage," which he employs. He states that, "A 'composition' for me forms sentence structures within a scenario of beginning, middle and end. Very much the way Picasso uses a rectangle as a ready-made protagonist. With assemblage there is no continuity of fitting the parts together as words in a sentence or paragraph." Feldman, Morton, *Give My Regards to Eighth Street*, 196.

Chapter Three

Large-scale Structure of *Piano and String Quartet*

This chapter will describe the large-scale structure of *Piano and String Quartet;* the next three chapters will address the subcomponents of the structure. As will be shown, *Piano and String Quartet* can be divided into three parts, designated A, B, and C (figure 3.1). The duration of the complete work in eighth-note values is 8,814.5. The duration of the respective parts in eighth-note values is 815 (9 percent of the total), 3,932.5 (45 percent), and 4,067 (46 percent).

Although the structure is tripartite, this is not a ternary form in the classical sense. Each part is distinctive and, in particular, Part C is not a recapitulation or variation of Part A. The respective parts are distinguishable by

	Part A	Part B	Part C
Measures	1-121	122-506	507-810
(Duration in 8th notes)	(815)	(3,932.5)	(4,067)
Texture	Piano and Strings Simultaneous	Instruments Alone, Dovetail, Antiphonal, Simultaneous	Antiphonal
Foreground Instrument	Piano	Piano and Strings	Strings

Figure 3.1. Large-scale Structure of Piano and String Quartet

contrasting textures and the foreground/background relationships among the instruments (i.e., whether piano or strings are in the foreground). In addition, there is distinctive pitch and harmonic material associated with each part, which helps to give each its particular identity. However, within each part there is also pitch/harmonic material that either foreshadows the material of subsequent parts or echoes material from preceding parts. There also are common elements among the pitch/harmonic materials of all three parts that contribute to the coherence of the composition. It is for these factors that the first 121 measures are deemed a distinct part, despite its much shorter duration in comparison to the other two parts.

The following analysis of the large-scale structure of *Piano and String Quartet* will focus on two criteria: texture and foreground/background relationships. The pitch and harmonic material will be described in detail in the succeeding three chapters.

PART A (M. 1–121)

The texture of Part A is Piano and Strings Simultaneous, and the instrument in the foreground is the piano. The 15 repetitions of the initial piano broken hexachord and its inversion over mm. 1–30 create a sense of stasis sonically, which is reinforced by the slow tempo and very quiet dynamics described earlier. Feldman was purposeful and intentional about his use of stasis. "I like to take repetition and develop it, I like to take variation and make a stasis rather than continual variation, and repetition is stasis."[1]

The way he manipulates this sense of stasis will be described in the detailed analysis in the section on the Part A subcomponents in the next chapter. However, it seems clear that stasis is the characteristic sonic hallmark that begins Part A.

TEXTURE

The texture of Part A is almost exclusively Piano and Strings Simultaneous. Of the 121 measures in this part, 109 exemplify this texture, generally in a two-bar pattern. In the first bar of the pattern, the instruments play simultaneously, starting on the downbeat of the measure and sustained through the bar line; in the second bar, the strings have dropped out and the sound of the piano decays.[2] This is true regardless of the number of strings playing (see figure 2.12 above and Foreground/Background discussion below). Consequently, the sonic contrast between piano and strings—particularly the decay in the piano—is established from the outset.

There are, however, four brief passages that can be identified as having distinctly different textures—Dovetail in two passages and Piano Alone in two passages—foreshadowing some of the textures in Part B. These will be described in detail in chapter 4.

FOREGROUND/BACKGROUND

In Part A, the piano is clearly established as foreground from the beginning and continues throughout. First, the piano plays a completely broken hexachord that is repeated five times over the first 10 measures. This is followed by the same hexachord, now partially broken, repeated five times over the next 10 measures. Finally, the same hexachord, now inverted and partially broken, is repeated five times over the next 10 measures. As noted above, the piano sounds in one measure and continues through the decay in the following measure, while the strings sound only in the first of those alternating measures. This pattern is present throughout Part A with only a few exceptions (i.e., mm. 68–69, 83–86, 99–100, and 118–121). Thus, on the basis of repetition and duration, the sound of the piano clearly predominates as the foreground in Part A.

PART B (MM. 122–506)

Part B stands in stark contrast with Part A. Where Part A was marked by a single overriding texture—Piano and Strings Simultaneous—Part B is comprised of five different textures and, within each texture, two to five variants of that texture. Where the piano had the foreground in Part A, the foreground moves from the piano at the beginning of Part B—as a "continuation" of Part A—to the strings at the end of Part B—as a preparation for Part C. Part B also contrasts with Part A in terms of the level of activity. The range of textures and the alternation of instruments in the foreground make Part B much more active and varied than Part A, creating a subtle sense of instability in comparison with the stasis of Part A. The resolution of this instability occurs in Part C.

Given the increased activity level, range of textures, and the foreground evolution from piano to strings, Part B could be considered functionally as a "working-through" of the composition that moves it from Part A to Part C.

TEXTURE

The five types of texture are all present in Part B: Piano Alone; Piano and Strings Simultaneous, Antiphonal, and Dovetail; and Strings Alone. In fact, where stasis is the sonic hallmark of Part A, mutability is the sonic hallmark of Part B.

Just as the first 30 measures of Part A set its textural framework, so do the first 30 measures of Part B, in which all five textures appear. The Dovetail texture opens Part B immediately at mm. 122–125 (figure 2.6, chapter 2).[3] The Piano and Strings Simultaneous texture first appears at mm. 127–130, Antiphonal at mm. 131–135, Piano Alone at mm. 145–146, and Strings Alone at m. 151 (figure 3.2).

Each of the textures appears in various forms—as many as five versions. For the sake of brevity, two sets of examples will be given: one for Piano Alone and one for Strings Alone. The Piano Alone texture may involve a specific set of single pitches that operate as a cell, as single chords fully broken, and as repeated pairs of fully broken chords (figure 3.3, figure 3.2(c)).

The Strings Alone texture appears in five different forms: as a single unbroken tetrachord, as a pair of unbroken tetrachords, as a broken tetrachord, as an echo of the piano cell (see figure 2.1, chapter 2), and, most uniquely in the composition, as a long single-note gesture in the cello that appears five times in Part B and nowhere else in the composition (figure 3.4; figure 2.9, chapter 2).

(a) (b)

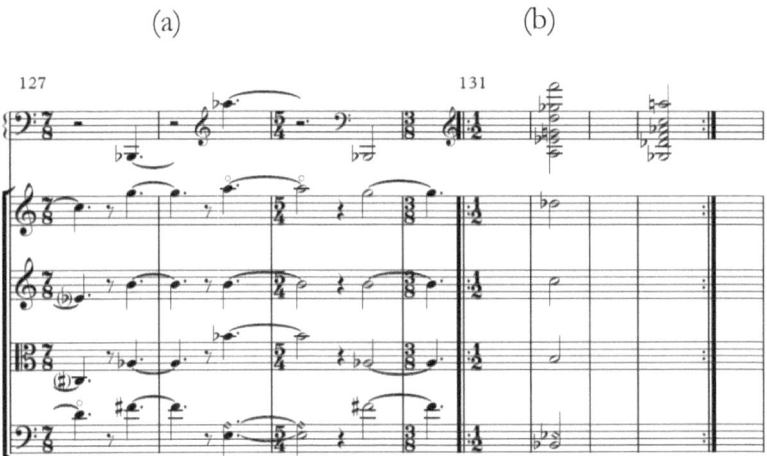

(c) (d)

Figure 3.2. Morton Feldman *Piano and String Quartet*
© Copyright 1985 by Universal Edition (London) Ltd., London / UE17972

Figure 3.3. Morton Feldman *Piano and String Quartet*

© Copyright 1985 by Universal Edition (London) Ltd., London / UE17972

Figure 3.4. Morton Feldman *Piano and String Quartet*
© Copyright 1985 by Universal Edition (London) Ltd., London / UE17972

FOREGROUND/BACKGROUND

In contrast to the predominance of the piano in Part A, over the course of Part B the foreground moves from the piano to the strings. The total duration of Part B is 3,932.5 eighth notes, with the duration of textures divided roughly into thirds. The total duration of the Piano Alone texture is 1,297 eighth notes; of the Strings Alone texture 1,259.5 eighth notes, and of the remaining three "shared" textures (Simultaneous, Antiphonal, and Dovetail) 1,376 eighth notes (figure 3.5).

On the surface, the foreground appears to be balanced about equally between the piano and strings in Part B overall. However, a closer look at the sections of Part B illustrates how the balance shifts from the piano to the strings. This is seen most clearly in comparing the durations of the Piano Alone and the Strings Alone textures. In Sections 1 and 2, the Piano Alone texture has durations of almost twice that of the Strings Alone texture (e.g., 468 vs. 281.5 eighth notes in Section 1). This is reversed in Section 3, in which the Strings Alone texture has a duration of more than twice that of the Piano Alone texture (i.e., 709 vs. 330 eighth notes). Where the piano is in the foreground in Sections 1 and 2, the strings have clear predominance in Section 3.

Texture	Part B Sections			Total
	Section 1 (mm. 122–244)	Section 2 (mm. 245–369)	Section 3 (mm. 370–506)	
Piano Alone	468	499	330	1297
Simultaneous, Antiphonal, and Dovetail	435	399	542	1376
Strings Alone	281.5	269	709	1259.5
Total	1184.5	1167	1581	3932.5

Figure 3.5. Part B: Section Durations in 8th Notes by Texture

PART C (MM. 507–810)

Stasis is the overriding sonic character of Part C. While this is evident in the music, so is it from Feldman's own words.

> ... this *String Quartet and Piano* [sic] is a perfect example [of stasis], in a sense, where I take repetition and I develop the repetition, essentially, with just two chords for a very, very long time.[4]
>
> Another aspect of why I am so fond of the piece is that the last half hour ... is really the isolating and re-orchestrating and the re-registration of just two chords, one after another, the same chords, where I just invert the chord.[5]

In fact, the two chords to which Feldman refers are 1-2-1 and 2-1-2 tetrachords in the strings, never transposed, which will be discussed in detail in the analysis of Part C in chapter 6. However, texture and instrument in the foreground are still the underlying elements that demarcate the three main parts of the large-scale structure of *Piano and String Quartet*.

TEXTURE

The texture of Part C, overall, is Antiphonal. Although locally there appear to be other textures used (e.g., Instrument Alone, Dovetail), the sonic experience involves alternating patterns that border on a "call and response" design for the most part. This is established in the first seven measures of Part C, in which the piano and strings alternate (figure 3.6).

Figure 3.6. Morton Feldman *Piano and String Quartet*
© Copyright 1985 by Universal Edition (London) Ltd., London / UE17972

Large-scale Structure of *Piano and String Quartet*   43

The reiteration of the two tetrachords in the strings that first appears in mm. 509–511 lays the foundation for the stasis that is at the heart of Part C.[6] Reiteration of these two string tetrachords continues without interruption from m. 519 through m. 806, just four measures from the end of the *Piano and String Quartet*.

Overlaying this foundational stasis is the intermittent appearance of the piano answering the strings (figure 3.7). Even though the texture locally is Dovetail in this example, the overall sonic effect of the alternating repeated bars without and with piano, here and throughout Part C, is Antiphonal.

Figure 3.7. Morton Feldman *Piano and String Quartet*
© Copyright 1985 by Universal Edition (London) Ltd., London / UE17972

FOREGROUND/BACKGROUND

The strings are clearly in the foreground throughout Part C. First, the duration of the strings is greater. Of the 304 measures of Part C, the strings are sounded in 294, compared to 105 in which the piano is sounded. Second, repeated material is much greater and more consistent in the strings than in the piano. The same pair of string tetrachords is reiterated in all but nine measures of Part C, compared with the more variable material appearing only intermittently in the piano.

CONCLUSION

The preceding analysis, based on texture and instrument in the foreground, demonstrates that *Piano and String Quartet* has a tripartite structure. Each of the three parts is distinct and contrasts with the other two. An additional consideration—the relative stasis or instability of the respective parts—suggests how the work evolves across the three parts.

Part A is characterized by a single texture—Piano and Strings Simultaneous, with the piano continually in the foreground. The overall sonic effect of this single texture and continuing foreground instrument is stasis. Part B with its multitude of textures and the foreground about equally shared by piano and strings is marked by constant change and shifts that could be construed as a kind of instability. Part C, although apparently Antiphonal in texture, is marked by stasis sonically, which is created by the very extensive reiteration of the underlying two-tetrachord pattern in the strings. Thus, *Piano and String Quartet* evolves from the piano and stasis in Part A to the strings and stasis in Part C, with Part B being the unstable working-through process of that evolution.

NOTES

1. Feldman, Morton, *Morton Feldman in Middelburg*, ed. Raoul Mörchen, *Morton Feldman in Middelburg: Words on Music—Lectures and Conversations, Vol. 1* (Köln: Ed. MusikTexte, 2008), 338.
2. An important exception is at mm. 76–77, in which there is no intervening empty measure, a foreshadowing of the attenuated rate of soundings that begin in m. 83 (see chapter 4, figures 4.10 and 4.11).
3. Although there is Dovetail texture in mm. 118–121, this analysis considers it a transition passage from Part A based on the pitch and harmonic content, which shifts to a new area at m. 122.
4. Feldman, Morton, *Morton Feldman in Middelburg*, 338.
5. Ibid., 466.
6. It should be noted that Feldman provides a foreshadowing of this two-chord pattern toward the end of Part B in m. 458 and mm. 479–485.

Chapter Four

Detailed Analysis of Part A

OVERVIEW

Stated in the most fundamental terms, *Piano and String Quartet* evolves in three mutually supportive ways: texturally, instrumentally, and harmonically.[1] The texture and instrumentation of the respective parts (regarding foreground/background design specifically) were discussed in chapter 3. In this and the next two chapters, the structure of each of the three parts will be analyzed individually and in greater detail. In the concluding chapter 7, the three parts will be considered as a whole.

In examining the details of the respective parts, the pitch/interval design will be considered first, then its temporal structure, focusing on duration and meter. Finally, the interaction among all of these parameters will be considered. The analysis will show the clear evolution from Part A, in which a single hexachord in the piano predominates as foreground, to Part C, in which a pair of tetrachords in the strings predominates as foreground. The analysis also will discuss how Feldman employs duration and meter as a propelling force. Tempo is constant throughout the composition (i.e., quarter note equals MM. 55.4). As such, duration will be expressed in terms of aggregates of eighth notes.

PART A (MM. 1–121)

Part A is comprised of five sections, with a total duration of 815 eighth notes. These are designated Section 1, 2, 3, 4, and 5 (figure 4.1). These sections are determined by the changes in the chordal material in the

Section	1	2	3	4	5
Measure	1–30	31–55	56–76	77–100	100–121
Duration (8th notes)	239	155	142	153	126
	815				
Percentage	29%	19%	17%	19%	15%

Figure 4.1. Overall Structure of Part A by Section and Duration in 8th Notes

piano, the foreground instrument of Part A, supported by an increase in density of the string sonorities within and across the sections.

Through a section-by-section analysis, it will be demonstrated that: (1) the rate of activity in the piano increases over the successive sections; (2) the density of string sonorities (i.e., pitch and interval content) increases from single notes or dyads to tetrachords within and across the sections; and (3) the duration of successive sections (and their respective subsections) generally decreases, creating what will be referred to as an increase in "pacing."

Changes in duration are achieved primarily through the manipulation of meter and the number of piano and string soundings per section.[2] Meter is not used to establish a continuing ictus, but rather to impact the duration of instrumental sounds. In fact, the absence of a sense of ictus is a characteristic of *Piano and String Quartet* and much, if not all, of Feldman's other music.

PITCH AND HARMONIC MATERIAL

Piano

The harmonic material of the piano part consists mainly of seven hexachords. These are designated Hexachords I–VII (figure 4.2). Inversions are indicated with subdivisions designated by lower-case letters (e.g., Ia, Ib). Although there are a few exceptions, the typical articulation for each hexachord is as a fully or partially rolled—or "broken"—chord.[3] Transpositions have a superscript indicating the distance in semitones from the initial form of the hexachord. The relative presence and importance of each hexachord is indicated by its total duration. These conventions will be used throughout the analysis.

Detailed Analysis of Part A 47

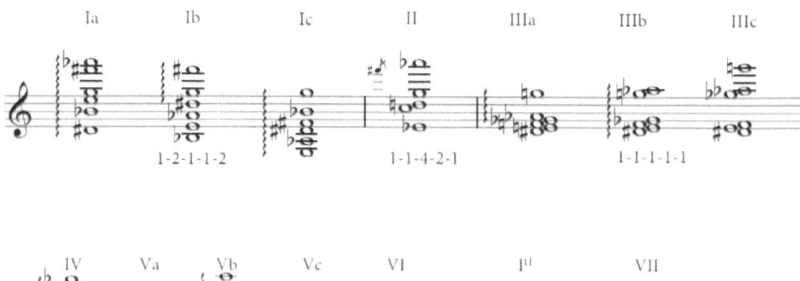

Figure 4.2. Hexachords in the Piano

Hexachord I is the predominant piano sonority in Part A (figure 4.3). With a total duration of 390 eighth notes, it comprises 48 percent of the 815 eighth-note duration of Part A. It is the first hexachord to be heard in the piece and the sole hexachord of Section 1, repeated 15 successive times, 10 in its initial form and then five in an inversion. It is also the only transposed hexachord in Part A.

Durations in 8th notes (Number of times sounded)	Pitch Content												Interval Content
	0	1	2	3	4	5	6	7	8	9	10	11	
	C	C#	D	D#	E	F	F#	G	G#	A	A#	B	
Hexachords													
I* 380 (27x)				D#	E		F#	G	G#		A#		1-2-1-1-2
390 (28x) 10 (1x)					E	F		G	G#	A		B	1-2-1-1-2^{t1}
II 112 (9x)	C		D	D#			F#	G	G#				1-1-4-2-1
III 150 (14X)				D#	E	F	F#	G	G#				1-1-1-1-1
IV 24 (2x)				D#	E		F#	G	G#			B	1-2-1-1-3
V 53 (5x)	C				E	F		G	G#			B	1-2-1-3-1
VI 28 (2x)		C#		D#	E	F	F#	G					2-1-1-1-1
VII 14 (1x)	C			D#	E	F		G					3-1-1-2*
Single Pitches													
24 (2x)								G					
20 (2x)							F#						

*Piano hexachords are identified by their Roman numeral designation and interval content.

Figure 4.3. Part A—Piano Hexachords and Single Pitches

Figure 4.4. Morton Feldman *Piano and String Quartet*

© Copyright 1985 by Universal Edition (London) Ltd., London / UE17972

Another prominent recurring sound in Part A is a two-note whole-step cell—F♯6-A♭6—a component of both Hexachords Ia and II (figure 4.4). Because the pitches of these hexachords are rolled ("broken"), the notes F♯6-A♭6 are heard sequentially. These notes are the last sounded, the highest in register, and separated by about an octave from the next note below (i.e., G5). Moreover, they are repeated 10 consecutive times over the first 20 measures. These factors make this cell quite distinctive. It becomes deeply ingrained as an aural guidepost that helps mark the sections of Part A.

Hexachords II and III also figure prominently in Part A. Hexachord III is second in prevalence, with a total duration of 150 eighth notes. Hexachord II is third, with a total duration of 112 eighth notes. The combined total duration of Hexachords I, II, and III is 652 eighth notes, or 80 percent of the duration of Part A. The remaining four hexachords are heard much less frequently, with total durations ranging from 14 to 53 eighth notes.

There is a high degree of overlap in pitch class content between Hexachord I and the other hexachords. This suggests that they all are variants—to greater and lesser degrees—of Hexachord I. However, Hexachord II is the closest to Hexachord Ia, based on three factors. First, the lowest pitch (D♯4/E♭4) and the upper three pitches (G5, F♯6, A♭6) of both hexachords are identical. Second, the pitches in the middle of these two hexachords are relatively close in range, moving either up one whole step (B♭4 to C5) or down one whole step (E5 to D5).[4] Finally, the aforementioned whole-step cell (F♯6-A♭6) is an element of only these two hexachords in Part A. The analysis below will demonstrate how Feldman uses the aural kinship between Hexachords Ia and II to divide Part A into sections.

Strings

The pitch and harmonic material of the strings in Part A consists of single notes, dyads, a single trichord, and tetrachords (figure 4.5). Pitch content

Durations in 8th notes (Number of times sounded)	Pitch Content												Interval Content
	0	1	2	3	4	5	6	7	8	9	10	11	
	C	C#	D	D#	E	F	F#	G	G#	A	A#	B	
Single Pitches													
32 (4x)		C#											
10 (2x)			D										
12 (2x)				D#									
28 (4x)										A			
28 (5x)												B	
Dyads													
51 (6x)	C	C#											1
12 (1x)		C#	D										1
18 (3x)										A	A#		1
22 (3x)	C											B	1
64 (11x)	C		D										2
Trichord													
12 (1x)	C	C#										B	1-1
Tetrachords													
32 (4x)	C	C#	D									B	1-1-1
60 (7x) 28 (3x)	C									A	A#	B	1-1-1^{T10}
8 (1x)	C	C#		D#								B	1-1-2
14 (2x)							F#	G	G#			B	1-1-3
8 (1x)	C						F#	G	G#				1-1-4
9 (2x)					E					A	A#	B	1-1-5
12 (2x)				D	D#	F	F#						1-2-1
24 (4x) 12 (2x)		C#	D		E	F							1-2-1^{T11}
8 (1x)		C#		D#						A	A#		1-3-2
8 (1x)			D		E					A	A#		1-4-2
6 (1x)	C		D							A		B	2-1-2
8 (1x)			D				F#	G	G#				4-1-1

Figure 4.5. Part A—String Single Notes, Dyads, Trichord, and Tetrachords

sounded in the string parts is generally different from the pitch collection sounded in the piano, with a few exceptions in which the piano and strings simultaneously play the same pitch class. Single notes and dyads are designated by their assigned pitch-class numbers, and the trichord and tetrachords by their interval content. Dyads and tetrachords are the predominant sonorities in the strings in Part A, with total durations of 167 eighth notes and 153 eighth notes, respectively.

In general, the strings move from single notes or dyads to tetrachords within subsections and across the respective sections of Part A. This increase in pitch/interval density helps propel Part A.

SECTION-BY-SECTION ANALYSIS OF PART A

Section 1 (mm. 1–30)

Section 1 has a total duration of 239 eighth notes and is comprised of three subsections (figure 4.6). Over the course of the three subsections, two elements work to subtly intensify the music. First, the speed of activity increases; that is, the duration of each successive subsection decreases while the number of soundings of piano and strings per subsection is constant. Second, the density of the string sonorities generally increases within and across the three successive subsections, from a single note or dyad to tetrachords. These elements also help demarcate the sections of Part A.

A two-bar pattern is established in Section 1 that typifies Part A. It consists of a measure in which a piano hexachord sounds (simultaneously with strings), alternating with one in which the piano hexachord decays (alone). The sonic experience of decay is an important element of *Piano and String Quartet*, which is heightened by the manipulation of meter within this two-bar framework.

The piano material in Section 1 is limited to Hexachord I, varied by articulation and inversion. First, Hexachord Ia is sounded fully rolled (mm. 1–10). Next, Hexachord Ia is sounded partially rolled (mm. 11–20). Finally, Hexachord Ib—an inversion of Hexachord I—is sounded, partially rolled (mm. 21–30). The character of Hexachord Ib clearly differentiates it from Ia. Its register is lower by about a perfect 4th and the familiar F#6-Ab6 whole-step cell is noticeably absent, now replaced by G5-F#6, a

Section 1–239 Eighth Notes (mm. 1–30)

	Subsection 1a – 93 eighth notes (mm. 1–10)	Subsection 1b – 81 eighth notes (mm. 11–20)	Subsection 1c – 65 eighth notes (mm. 21–30)
Piano	Ia 1-2-1-1-2 3,4,6,7,8,10	Ia (partially rolled) 1-2-1-1-2 3,4,6,7,8,10	Ib 1-2-1-1-2 3,4,6,7,8,10

Piano Hexachord / Interval / Pitch class

Strings	→	→	→	→	→	→	→	→	→	→	→	→
Pitch class	0 1	0 1 11		0 1 2 11		0 2	9	2 **6** 7 **8**		0 **6** 7 **8**	2 **3** 5 **6**	1 2 **4** 5	9	0 1 2 11
Interval	1	1-1		1-1-1	1			4-1-1		1-1-4	1-2-1	1-2-1-T^{u}		1-1-1

Legend: $0 = C$, $1 = C\#/Db$, $2 = D$, $3 = D\#/Eb$, $4 = E$, $5 = F$, $6 = F\#/Gb$, $7 = G$, $8 = G\#/Ab$, $9 = A$, $10 = A\#/Bb$, $11 = B$; **X** = common tones between strings and piano; ↓ = sounding.

Figure 4.6. Part A, Section 1: Piano and Strings—Durations and Harmonic Analysis by Pitch Class and Interval, by Subsection

major seventh. Each of these manifestations of Hexachord I is repeated five successive times, respectively. These three sets of hexachord repetitions, given their associated changes in articulation and inversion, help define the three subsections of Section 1 (1a, 1b, and 1c).

Manipulation of meter also underpins the structure of Section 1. First, it gives shape to the subsections. Specifically, the meter in each sounding measure in subsection 1a is 3/2, in subsection 1b is 2/2, and in subsection 1c, 3/4.[5] At a higher level, changes in meter, by their effect on duration—and thus on pacing—give shape to Section 1 overall. With subsection durations of 93, 81, and 65 eighth notes respectively, the rate of activity intensifies as the music progresses across Section 1. The rate of activity then decreases at the beginning of Section 2, with its meter of 2/2 in the initial sounding measures. This larger-scale intensification and lessening of pace through the manipulation of meter helps distinguish between the sections and, thus, is a key factor contributing to form.

In the string part, the manipulation of pitch/interval density is a central element. It is realized in the pattern of increasing density of the string sonorities that is employed within and across the sections of Part A. For example, subsection 1a begins with semitone dyads in the strings (0,1), expands to trichords, also consisting of semitones (11,0,1), and then expands further to tetrachords consisting of semitones (11,0,1,2). This progressive buildup of textural density acts as an animating force, contrasting with the relative stasis of the repeated Hexachord I in the piano. At the same time, the four component pitch classes in the strings—0, 1, 2, and 11—are established as a group of central pitches comprising what becomes a familiar 1-1-1 tetrachord.

At the end of subsection 1a, this general pattern begins again with a semitone dyad (1,2). At the beginning of subsection 1b, the size of the dyad expands to a whole tone (0,2), and then leads to a series of tetrachords, all punctuated somewhat by single notes (9) and (3). The series begins with new tetrachords 4-1-1 and 1-1-4, noteworthy in their sharing three pitch classes with piano Hexachord I (i.e., 6,7,8). Subsection 1c continues with the introduction of tetrachord 1-2-1 (2,3,5,6) and its half-step transposition $1\text{-}2\text{-}1^{t11}$ (1,2,4,5).[6] Thus, as the string density increases, there also is movement away from the central pitch collection established in subsection 1a. The 1-2-1 tetrachord foreshadows Part C, in which the strings only sound 1-2-1 and 2-1-2 tetrachords. Subsection 1c ends with a return of the very first string tetrachord of Section 1: 1-1-1 (11,0,1,2). The return of this tetrachord and pitch collection functions as a kind of cadence, reinforcing the sense that Section 1 is ending.[7]

Section 2 (mm. 31–55)

Section 2 is similar to Section 1 in having three subsections demarcated primarily by changes in the piano hexachords, and in the density of the string sonorities thickening over its course (figure 4.7). In contrast, the overall pace, harmonic activity, and hexachord variety are all greater in Section 2.

The duration of Section 2 is 155 eighth notes, compared with 239 eighth notes for Section 1. The increased pace of activity within Section 2 is also reflected within each of its three subsections, with durations of 56 eighth notes, 48 eighth notes, and 51 eighth notes, respectively. These all are shorter in duration than the briefest subsection of Section 1 (i.e., 65 eighth notes in subsection 1c). The shorter durations are due primarily to the four rather than five hexachord soundings per subsection and to the manipulation of meter.

Just as Hexachord I in its various manifestations defined the subsections of Section 1, different hexachords are used to define the subsections of Section 2. Subsection 2a begins with three soundings of newly introduced Hexachord II followed by one of Hexachord Ia; as such, the now familiar F♯6-A♭6 cell is sounded four times successively. Since this cell was not present at the end of Section 1, its presence at the start of Section 2 brings a sense of return, an echo of the beginning of the composition. Together with its fresh pitch content and a new kind of articulation (i.e., the grace-note "broken one-note"), Hexachord II clearly suggests the beginning of a new section.

Subsection 2b is defined by a change to new Hexachords IIIa and IIIb. It both resembles and contrasts with subsection 2a. Three soundings of Hexachord IIIa are followed by one sounding of Hexachord IIIb. This repeats the three-sounding/one-sounding pattern of the two hexachords of subsection 2a, but at a subtly increased pace.[8]

There also are striking sonic differences between the two subsections. First, the F♯6-A♭6 cell so prominent in subsection 2a is noticeably absent in 2b. Instead, the two highest notes of Hexachord IIIa are A♭4-G5 (a ma-

Piano	Section 2–155 Eighth Notes (mm. 31–55)			
	Subsection 2a–56 eighth notes (mm. 31–38) 43 eighth notes	Subsection 2b–48 eighth notes (mm. 39–46) 38 eighth notes		Subsection 2c–51 eighth notes (mm. 47–55)
		13 eighth notes	10 eighths	
	II	**Ia**	**IIIa**	**IIIb**	**Ib**
Hexachord	1-1-4-2-1	1-2-1-1-2	1-1-1-1	1-1-1-1-1	1-2-1-1
Interval	→	→	→	→	→	→
Pitch class	0,2,3,6,7,8	3,4,6,7,8,10	3,4,5,6,7,8	3,4,5,6,7,8	3,4,6,7,8,10
				→	→
Strings					
Pitch class	11	0	0	0	9	1	0	2
	1	2	2	2	10	2	1	3
						4	2	5
						5	11	**6**
Interval	→	2	2	2	1	1-2-1ᵀᴴ	1-1-1	1-2-1

Figure 4.7. Part A, Section 2: Piano and Strings—Durations and Harmonic Analysis by Pitch Class and Interval, by Subsection

jor 7th) and of IIIb are its inversion G5-A♭5 (a semitone). Not only is the whole-step cell replaced, but the register of the two top notes is an octave or more lower as well. Second, the hexachords in the respective subsections have dramatically contrasting sounds. The greater span (about two and one-half octaves) and larger intervals of Hexachords Ia and II result in an open, expansive sound. On the other hand, the much smaller span (about a major 10th) and mostly semitone intervals of Hexachords IIIa and IIIb result in a constricted, cluster-like sonority.

Subsection 2c, like subsection 1c, is comprised solely of Hexachord 1b, which sonically is open and expansive. Thus, there is a clear progression in the overall sound of the piano as it moves across Section 2: from a widely spaced sonority in subsection 2a, to constricted in subsection 2b, to widely spaced again in subsection 2c. The overall effect is a subtle tightening and release of tension.[9]

In the strings, the increasing density of pitch/interval sonorities helps propel Section 2, just as it does in Section 1. Single notes progress to dyads across the first two subsections, moving to three tetrachords in subsection 2c: 1-2-1^{t11} (1,2,4,5), 1-1-1 (11,0,1,2), and 1-2-1 (2,3,5,6).[10] These are the same three tetrachords that were sounded at the end of Section 1, paralleling their use to signal the end of a section. Although the order of these tetrachords is changed, blunting the cadential effect of the return of the 1-1-1 trichord, the emphasis on the 1-2-1 tetrachords remains present to foreshadow Part C.

Section 3 (mm. 56–76)

Section 3 is clearly reminiscent of Section 2; it is similar in its tripartite structure, piano hexachords, and increase in density of string sonorities. Like Section 2, Section 3 has a faster pace than its predecessor. Its total duration is 142 eighth notes, with decreasing subsection durations of 58, 48, and 36 eighth notes, respectively (figure 4.8).

Evidence of the connection between Sections 2 and 3 is seen first in the series of piano hexachords. Although not identical, they are comprised of much of the same material. Subsection 3a, like subsection 2a, begins with Hexachord II (with an inversion of Hexachord I now interposed), then moves to Hexachord III in subsection 3b (with the order of IIIa and IIIb now reversed), and closes in subsection 3c with Hexachords Ia (replac-

Section 3–142 Eighth Notes (mm. 56–76)

	Subsection 3a–58 eighth notes (mm. 56–63)			Subsection 3b–48 eighth notes (mm. 64–71)			Subsection 3c–36 eighth notes (mm. 72–76)	
	28 eighth notes	13 eighth notes	17 eighth notes	12 eighth notes		36 eighth notes	12 eighths	24 eighth notes
Piano								
Hexachord	II	Ib	II	IIIb		IIIa	Ia	IV
Interval	1-1-4-2-1	1-2-1-2	1-1-4-2-1	1-1-1-1		1-1-1-1	1-2-1-2	1-2-1-1-3
Pitch class	0,2,3,6,7,8	3,4,6,7,8,10	0,2,3,6,7,8	3,4,5,6,7,8		3,4,5,6,7,8	3,4,6,7,8,10	3,4,6,7,8,11
	→	→	→	→	→	→	→	→
Strings								
Pitch class	1	9	11	9 10	0 2	no strings w/piano	0 2	0 1	2 4 9 10
Interval	1			1	2	2	2	1	1-4-2

Figure 4.8. Part A, Section 3: Piano and Strings—Durations and Harmonic Analysis by Pitch Class and Interval, by Subsection

ing Ib) and IV (its close variant).[11] In the strings, the pattern of increasing pitch/interval density occurs again, beginning with single notes in subsection 3a, expanding to dyads in subsection 3b, and concluding with newly introduced tetrachord 1-4-2 (9, 10, 2, 4) at the end of subsection 3c. Despite the obvious strength of the parallels between the two sections, Feldman would view these not as variations in the usual "theme and variations" sense, but as different perspectives on the material being used.

> ... the minute you say "variation" it has a connotation for me. For example, in *Crippled Symmetry* the way I manipulate my four notes over in different ways. If I thought I was *varying* it there would be no piece. But I'm hearing it in a different light, in a different context as it moves [like the juxtaposition of forms in a Calder mobile] ... I'm not *hearing* it as variation.[12,13]

Most importantly, this is the culmination of a progressive process across Sections 1, 2, and 3. While continuity has been established through repetition and variance of pitch/interval materials, the pace has quickened, with the total durations of sections decreasing from 239 to 155 to 142 eighth notes, respectively. There has been an associated increase in harmonic activity across the three sections in piano and strings, concluding with new Hexachord IV in the piano and new tetrachord 1-4-2 in the strings. Together, these forces subtly push the music forward to Section 4.

Section 4 (mm. 77–100)

Section 4 is the high point of Part A (figure 4.9). It has four subsections, rather than the three of the earlier sections, and stands out from the other sections in many ways. It is marked by instability in comparison to the other sections, beginning with the disruption of the well-established two-bar sounding measure/decaying measure pattern. It also has the greatest activity in the piano, extremes in the register placement of the piano hexachords, the first appearance of single notes in the piano, and the greatest number of successive string tetrachords. Especially striking is the introduction of the dovetail texture after hearing only the simultaneous texture throughout Sections 1–3. Unlike Sections 1, 2, 3, and 5, which are built around Hexachord I or II and the prominent use of the F#6-A♭6 cell, Section 4 is built around newly introduced Hexachord V and the F#6-A♭6 cell is completely absent.

	Section 4–153 Eighth Notes (mm. 77–100)							
	Subsection 4a—48 eighth notes (mm. 77–82)			Subsection 4b—36 eighth notes (mm. 83–86)			Subsection 4c—44 eighth notes (mm. 87–92)		Subsection 4d–25 eighths (mm. 93–100)			
	16 eighth notes	16 eighths	16 eighths	18 eighths	10 eighths	8 eighths	24 eighth notes	20 eighth notes	12 eighths	6 8ths	7 8ths
Piano											
Hexachord	Va	Ic	VI	IIIa IIIc	I^{T1}	Vb	Single Note 7	Single Note 6	IIIa	Ic	Va
Interval	1-2-1-3-1	1-2-1-1-2	2-1-1-1	1-1-1-1	1-2-1-1-2	1-2-1-3-1	→	→	1-1-1-1-1	1-2- 1-1- 1	1-2- 1-3- 1
Pitch class	0,4,5,7,8,11 →	3,4,6,7, 8, 10 →	1,3,4,5,6,7 →	3,4,5,6,7,8 →	4,5,7,8,9,11 →	0,4,5,7,8,11 →			3,4,5,6,7,8 →		
Strings											
Pitch class	**0**	0	0	0	1	**0**	6	4	0	0	
	1	1	11	1	3	9	7	9	2	1	
				2	**9**	10	8	10	2		
				11	10	**11**	11	11			
Interval	1	1	1	1-1-1 1-1-2	1-3-2	1-1-1^{t60}	1-1-3	1-1-5	2 2	1	

Figure 4.9. Part A, Section 4: Piano and Strings—Durations and Harmonic Analysis by Pitch Class and Interval, by Subsection

Detailed Analysis of Part A 59

The piano and string sonorities work in tandem to define the structure of Section 4. Piano Hexachord Va sets its boundaries, sounded at the beginning of subsection 4a and the end of subsection 4d. Its inversion, Hexachord Vb, is sounded in the middle, in m. 86, separating subsection 4b from the single notes of 4c.

The string sonorities similarly mark the boundaries of Section 4. Dyads heard in earlier sections are sounded at the beginning of subsection 4a (0,1 and 11,0) and at the end in subsection 4d (0,2 and 0,1). Subsection 4b continues to reflect back to earlier sections sounding the original form of tetrachord 1-1-1 (11,0,1,2), which is then incrementally transformed through a series of tetrachords into its T^{10} transposition (9,10,11,0).

Also helping define the structure of Section 4 is the disruption of the prevailing two-bar duration scheme, starting in measure 77 (figure 4.10). This abrupt beginning of a new pattern of sounding and alternating "decay" measures, together with the appearance of new Hexachord Va, clearly establishes Section 4 and sets it apart.

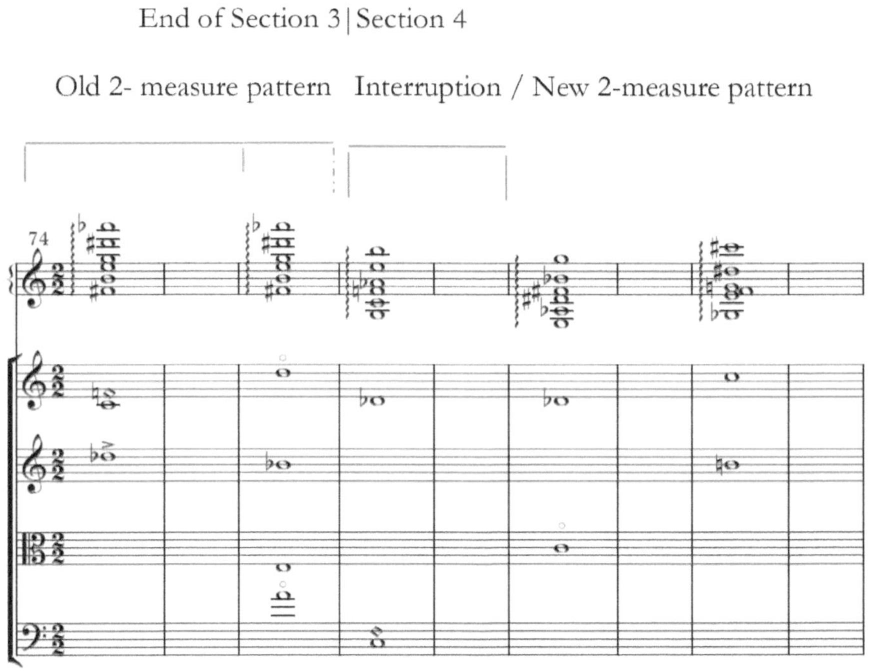

End of Section 3 | Section 4

Old 2- measure pattern   Interruption / New 2-measure pattern

Figure 4.10. Morton Feldman *Piano and String Quartet*
© Copyright 1985 by Universal Edition (London) Ltd., London / UE17972

Shifts in register in the piano part also set Section 4 apart. Such changes not only add to the instability that characterizes Section 4, but also align with the other form-defining factors. A conspicuous example occurs at the start of the section. The sounding of Hexachord Va in m. 77 follows Hexachord IV—at the end of Section 3—with a resulting downward shift in register of about a major seventh.[14] This is the largest hexachord-to-hexachord shift in register up to this point in Part A. It is followed by the final downward shift in register to Hexachord Ic in m. 79, with initial note E3. Reaching this low turning point marks the consequential nature of Hexachord Ic in the piano; its pitches are likewise consequentially used in Part B to form a 2-1-1 string tetrachord that will be discussed in the analysis of that part in chapter 5.

The register of the hexachords now begins to rise in m. 81, moving to the highest point in all of Part A in m. 86 with the sounding of Hexachord Vb, spanning G4 to B6 (figure 4.11).

Figure 4.11. Morton Feldman *Piano and String Quartet*
© Copyright 1985 by Universal Edition (London) Ltd., London / UE17972

This dramatic shift in register is accompanied by a change in texture in mm. 83–86 with the introduction of "broken-ness" in the strings, simulating the rolled articulation and decay of the piano hexachords, adding another element of instability. This broken articulation is achieved by the alternation and overlapping of pairs of notes by pairs of string instruments. Together with the piano, the texture is changed from simultaneous to dovetail, both heightening the tension and foreshadowing the more extensive textural changes to come in Part B.

Detailed Analysis of Part A 61

From mm. 87–99, the piano returns, in stages, to its initial register at the end of Section 4, m. 99 (figure 4.12 continuing from figure 4.11). The strings return to the simultaneous texture, shrinking in density from tetrachords to semitone dyads.

Figure 4.12. Morton Feldman *Piano and String Quartet*
© Copyright 1985 by Universal Edition (London) Ltd., London / UE17972

Although it seems inappropriate with respect to Feldman's aesthetic to refer to Section 4 as a "climax" of Part A, it is clear that the music from Section 1 on has been steadily rising to this high point as a target and then falls away in transition to the next section. Register and harmonic material in the piano, together with texture, density, and pitch/interval material in the strings, and the interruption of the two-bar pattern, all align to define the shape of Section 4. They create a sense of instability, in stark contrast with the sections preceding Section 4. More importantly, Section 4 foreshadows the textural and harmonic instability of Part B, which will soon begin in m. 122.

Section 5 (mm. 101–121)

Section 5, like Section 3, is reminiscent of Section 2 (figure 4.13). It serves as both a return and transition, reiterating earlier material in somewhat abbreviated fashion, and foreshadowing material that will appear in Parts B and C. Section 5 is the shortest of the five sections of Part A. Accordingly, it seems appropriate to view it as a whole rather than divide it into subsections.

	Section 5 – 126 Eighth Notes (mm. 101-121)							
	24 eighth notes	8 eighths	12 eighths	24 eighth notes 12 eighths | 12 eighths		22 eighth notes	22 eighth notes 10 eighths | 12 eighths		14 eighths
				IIIb	IIIa	Ia	Vb	Vc	VII
Piano									
Hexachord	II	Ib	VI	1-1-1-1	1-1-1-1	1-2-1-2	1-2-1-3-1	1-2-1-3-1	3-1-1-2
Interval	1-1-4-2-1	1-2-1-1-2	2-1-1-1	3,4,5,6,7,8		3,4,6,7,8,10		0,4,5,7,8,11	0,3,(3),4,5,7
Pitch class	0,2,3,6,7,8	3,4,6,7,8,10	1,3,4,5,6,7	→	→	→	→	→	→
	→	→	→	9 10	2	0 2	**0** 9 10 **11**	**0** 9 10 **11**	**0** **11**
						0 2 9 11		**0** **11**	
Strings									
Pitch class	11	2	0 11						
	11								
Interval	→								
	11	2	1	1		2	1	1-1-1^{T10} 1-1-1^{T10}	1
						2-1-2			

Figure 4.13. Part A, Section 5: Piano and Strings—Durations and Harmonic Analysis by Pitch Class and Interval, by Subsection

Like Sections 2 and 3, Section 5 begins in the piano with Hexachord II, moves to Hexachords IIIb/IIIa, and returns to an inversion of Hexachord I. This final sounding of the all-important Hexachord Ia in m. 117 marks the end of Part A via the twice-repeated reference to the hexachord of its beginning. Section 5 closes with Hexachords Vb/Vc—a quick departing allusion to Section 4—and finally ends with new Hexachord VII.

This final hexachord in the piano in Part A is unique, as it appears nowhere else in the composition and is the only piano hexachord to have a pitch class doubled (i.e., pitch class 3—E♭3, D♯6). With these as its highest and lowest notes, extending over three full octaves, Hexachord VII has the greatest span of the other hexachords in Part A. But it also is a reference to other key hexachords, because pitch-class 3 is the lowest note of Hexachords Ia, II, IIIa, and IIIb, the predominant hexachords of Part A. Clearly, the deployment of Hexachord VII is one of Feldman's signals that something new is about to start.

In the strings, the previously seen general pattern of increasing pitch/interval density appears again. Single notes move to dyads and then to tetrachords.

Finally, the material of mm. 118–121 complete the transition to Part B. Tetrachord 1-1-1^{t10} returns in the strings, sounded in broken form, with dovetailed pairs of instruments in mm. 118–119, and dovetailed with piano Hexachords Vb and Vc as well (figure 4.14). Bringing back the dovetail texture is another allusion to Section 4, important also as preparation for the changes in texture that mark Part B.

Figure 4.14. Morton Feldman *Piano and String Quartet*
© Copyright 1985 by Universal Edition (London) Ltd., London / UE17972

SUMMARY

Overall, Part A represents a microcosm of the composition: from stasis to instability and, ultimately, the return to stasis. It is comprised of five sections generally increasing in pace. Sections 1–3 lead inexorably to Section 4, the high point of Part A. With their similar tripartite structures, focus on Hexachords Ia, Ib, and II, and prevalence of the F#6-A♭6 cell, the variances among Sections 1–3 can be considered as a set that exemplifies the subtle ways in which Feldman conceptualizes and manipulates his materials, looking at them from different angles and in different contexts. Section 4 contrasts with the other sections. It has four subsections rather than three, extreme shifts in register, new pitch/interval material in the piano and strings, no occurrence of the F#6-A♭6 cell, and a change from simultaneous to dovetail texture. Section 5, essentially a return of—or more accurately, a different turn on—the material of the first three, brings Part A to a close and serves as transition to Part B.

The increased pace of activity over the first three sections results from the successive lessening of duration and expansion of harmonic activity, particularly in the piano. This movement toward Section 4 is supported by the thickening density of the string pitch/interval material within and across sections. The increasing density of the string sonorities not only acts as a propulsive force in Part A, but has apparent tetrachord targets as well in Sections 2, 3, and 5, and beyond, including Part C.

Repetition and variance of material are the source of the stasis in Part A. These, together with manipulation of duration, the harmonic activity in the piano, and the density of the string sonorities, are the primary factors that, as Feldman would say, "keep it going."

NOTES

1. See chapter 2, note 8 on the terms "harmonic" and "harmonically" as used herein.

2. As mentioned earlier, the terms "sounding" and "sounded" are being used because Feldman intended the music to be "attackless."

3. In a letter sent to Aki Takahashi while working on *Piano and String Quartet*, Feldman wrote, "Never expected to write a piece with just broken chords!" See letter in appendix B.

4. Although Feldman rarely, if ever, mentioned classical voice leading as an element of his music, the movement of B♭4 to C5 and E5 to D5 is like upper and lower neighbors moving in contrary motion, another reason to view these two hexachords as closely related.

5. The meter of the decay measures is variable, decreasing and increasing in duration within subsections. For example, bars 2, 4, 6, 8, and 10 in subsection 1a have meters of 8/8, 7/8, 6/8, 5/8, and 7/8, respectively.

6. Feldman used transposition by half-step with intention, and a possibly "tonal/modulatory" connection: "I certainly use Stravinsky's half-step modulation. I use it all the time. You'll find it in this piece [i.e., *Piano and String Quartet*]."

Feldman, Morton, *Morton Feldman in Middelburg*, 468.

7. Feldman stated, while discussing *Piano and String Quartet*, that there were "keys" underlying some of his very late music: "Now do you think in 1986, in the age of polyphony, that there are keys? Well I wouldn't call them really keys but they are. . . . That first happened in *Triadic Memories,* when I do it one way and then in another key and in another key. And I was looking for what I would feel [was] the Utopia, the real key, the real home of the passage."

Feldman, Morton, *Morton Feldman in Middelburg*, 468.

8. The total duration of subsection 2b is 48 eighth-notes versus 56 eighth-notes in subsection 2a.

9. One might view this as a local example of the stasis-instability-stasis that marks the large-scale relationship among the composition's three parts.

10. Here Feldman reverses the order of the transposed 1-2-1 tetrachords from their respective positions in subsection 1c, another subtle example of a move away and then return to a "tonal center."

11. Hexachord IV is a close variant of Hexachord Ia, differing by one semitone in one pitch class only (i.e., B♭ becomes B); however, it does not have the F♯6-A♭6 cell.

12. Feldman, Morton, *Morton Feldman in Middelburg*, 76–78.

13. For this reason, the terms "variance" or "variant" will be used herein, rather than "variation."

14. The lowest notes of the respective hexachords are F♯4 and G3, perhaps a retrograde echo of the major seventh leaps of the upper two notes of Hexachords Ib and IIIa.

Chapter Five

Detailed Analysis of Part B

OVERVIEW

Part B is characterized by instability. This instability arises from the expanded diversity of pitch/interval material and textures. Some of its musical ideas are unique, some echo those of Part A, and some foreshadow and, indeed, engender Part C. Most notably, the function of Part B is transformative, moving the composition from the predominance of single piano hexachords in Part A to the predominance of a specific pair of string tetrachords in Part C.

The expanded diversity of harmonic material in the piano consists of 16 new hexachords, six pentachords, 10 tetrachords, and two trichords (figures 5.1, 5.2). In contrast, there are just seven hexachords in Part A.

Most of the harmonic material in the piano part is unique to Part B. The exceptions are Hexachords I, II, and V (from Part A), and Hexachords X and XXI, and Tetrachords 1-1-4, 1-2-1, and 2-1-2 (foreshadowing Part C). Further, transpositions occur much more frequently than in Part A: eight hexachords, two pentachords, four tetrachords, and one trichord have one or two transpositions. Only one piano hexachord in Part A was transposed.

Likewise, the number of string tetrachords heard in Part B increases. Where there were 10 different tetrachords in Part A, there are 14 in Part B, six of which having one to four transpositions (figure 5.3). Five of these string tetrachords are unique to Part B: 1-3-1, 2-1-1, 2-1-4, 2-3-2, and 3-1-1.

Durations in 8th notes (Number of times sounded)		Pitch Content												Interval Content
		0	1	2	3	4	5	6	7	8	9	10	11	
		C	C#	D	D#	E	F	F#	G	G#	A	A#	B	
VIII	15 (1x)		C#	D	D#	E	F		G					1-1-1-1-2
IX	20 (2x)	C		D	D#						A	A#	B	1-1-1-2-1
44 (4x)	24 (2x)	C	C#		D#	E						A#	B	1-1-1-2-1^{T1}
X	20 (2x)			D	D#	E	F				A	A#		1-1-1-4-1
135 (11x)	115 (9x)		C#	D	D#	E				G#	A			1-1-1-4-1^{T11}
XI	16 (2x)	C	C#		D#	E				G#			B	1-1-2-1-4
XII	11 (1x)	C		D		E			G			A#	B	1-1-2-2-3
II (Part A)	16 (2x)	C		D	D#			F#	G	G#				1-1-4-2-1
I (Part A)	104 (6x)			D	D#		F	F#	G		A			1-2-1-1-2^{T11}
224 (17x)	440 (32x)				D#	E		F#	G	G#		A#		1-2-1-1-2
	112 (9x)					E	F		G	G#	A		B	1-2-1-1-2^{T1}
XIII	12 (1x)				D#	E		F#	G		A	A#		1-2-1-2-1
V (Part A)	13 (1x)	C				E	F		G	G#			B	1-2-1-3-1
114 (9x)	101 (8x)	C	C#				F	F#		G#	A			1-2-1-3-1^{T1}
XIV	74 (8x)					E	F		G		A	A#	B	1-2-2-1-1
XV	49 (3x)			D	D#			F#	G	G#	A			1-3-1-1-1
68 (4x)	19 (1x)		C#	D			F	F#	G	G#				1-3-1-1-1^{T11}
XVI	48 (3x)		C#	D			F		G	G#		A#		1-3-2-1-2
70 (4x)	22 (1x)			D	D#			F#		G#	A		B	1-3-2-1-2^{T1}
XVII	16 (1x)	C	C#		D#	E					A		B	2-1-1-2-1
XVIII	74 (8x)			D		E		F#	G	G#		A#		2-2-1-1-2
176 (14x)	102 (6x)		C#		D#		F	F#	G		A			2-2-1-1-2^{T11}
XIX	68 (6x)		C#			E		F#		G#	A	A#		2-2-1-1-3
XX	63 (5x)		C#			E	F	F#	G	G#				3-1-1-1-1
XXI	18 (1x)	C	C#				F			G#		A#	B	3-2-1-1-1
XXII	6 (1x)			D			F		G	G#		A#	B	3-2-1-1-2
XXIII	57 (6x)				D#				G	G#	A	A#	B	4-1-1-1-1
86 (8x)	29 (2x)	C				E				G#	A	A#	B	4-1-1-1-1^{T1}

Figure 5.1. Part B—Piano Hexachords

Durations in 8th notes (Number of times sounded)		Pitch Content												Interval Content
		0	1	2	3	4	5	6	7	8	9	10	11	
		C	C#	D	D#	E	F	F#	G	G#	A	A#	B	
Pentachords														
Pent-I	31 (4x)		C#	D	D#			F#		A				1-1-3-3
Pent-II	15 (1x)					E	F			G#		A#	B	1-3-2-1
Pent-III	32 (4x)		C#	D	D#	E							B	2-1-1-1
60.5 (8x)	28.5 (4x)	C		D	D#	E	F							2-1-1-1^{T1}
Pent-IV	13 (1x)	C		D	D#		F		G					2-1-2-2
Pent-V	38 (4x)	C		D	D#		F			G#				2-1-2-3
73.5 (8x)	35.5 (4x)		C#		D#	E		F#			A			2-1-2-3^{T1}
Pent-VI	11 (1x)		C#		D#		F		G				B	2-2-2-2
Tetrachords														
Tet-I	37 (4x)					E	F	F#		G#				1-1-2
60 (6x)	23 (2x)								G	G#	A		B	1-1-2^{T3}
Tet-II	11 (1x)	C							G	G#	A			1-1-3
57 (3x)	46 (2x)	C	C#			E							B	1-1-3^{T4}
Tet-III	22 (2x)	C	C#				F						B	1-1-4
Tet-IV	64 (10x)						F	F#		G#	A			1-2-1
Tet-V	29 (2x)	C	C#			E	F							1-3-1
Tet-VI	28 (4x)					E	F					A#	B	1-5-1
68 (8x)	24 (2x)	C	C#					F#	G					1-5-1^{T2}
	16 (2x)		C#	D					G	G#				1-5-1^{T3}
Tet-VII	52 (8x)		C#	D		E							B	2-1-2
102 (12x)	12 (2x)	C		D	D#		F							2-1-2^{T1}
	38 (2x)	C	C#		D#							A#		2-1-2^{T11}
Tet-VIII	38 (2x)	C	C#				F					A#		2-1-4
Tet-IX	16 (1x)		C#		D#		F				A			2-2-4
Tet-X	38 (2x)	C	C#							G#			B	3-1-1
Trichords														
Tri-I	16 (1x)		C#									A#	B	1-2
Tri-II	54 (3x)	C	C#									A#		2-1
	44 (2x)	C	C#		D#									2-1^{T2}
Single Pitches														
	14 (2x)						F							
	9 (1x)									G#				
	20 (2x)											A#		

Figure 5.2. Part B—Piano Pentachords, Tetrachords, Trichords, and Single Pitches

Durations in 8th notes (Number of times sounded)		Pitch Content												Interval Content
		0	1	2	3	4	5	6	7	8	9	10	11	
		C	C#	D	D#	E	F	F#	G	G#	A	A#	B	
Tetrachords															
	6 (1x)	C	C#	D									B	1-1-1
	193 (30x)	C	C#	D	D#									1-1-1^{T1}
376 (64x)	14 (2x)		C#	D	D#	E								1-1-1^{T2}
	111 (24x)								G	G#	A	A#		1-1-1^{T8}
	52 (8x)	C	C#									A#	B	1-1-1^{T11}
	6 (1x)	C	C#		D#								B	1-1-2
	13 (2x)							F#	G	G#			B	1-1-3
33 (4x)	20 (2x)	C	C#			E							B	1-1-3^{T5}
	20 (1x)	C	C#				F						B	1-1-4
	11 (2x)					E					A	A#	B	1-1-5
68 (12x)	46 (8x)		C#	D	D#					G#				1-1-5^{T4}
	11 (2x)				D#					G#	A	A#		1-1-5^{T11}
	6 (1x)			D	D#		F	F#						1-2-1
	24 (4x)				D#	E		F#	G					1-2-^{T1}
117.5 (26x)	81.5 (20x)						F	F#		G#	A			1-2-1^{T3}
	6 (1x)		C#	D		E	F							1-2-1^{T11}
	50 (8x)			D	D#		F			G#				1-2-3
	75 (21x)						F	F#			A	A#		1-3-1
	18 (2x)	C		D						G#	A			1-3-2
26 (3x)	8 (1x)		C#		D#						A	A#		1-3-2^{T1}
	332 (15x)					E		F#	G	G#				2-1-1
	226 (34x)	C	C#		D#							A#		2-1-2^{T1}
280.5 (50x)	54.5 (15x)		C#	D		E							B	2-1-2^{T2}
	22 (1x)	C	C#				F					A#		2-1-4
	18 (3x)	C					F		G			A#		2-3-2
	20 (1x)	C	C#							G#			B	3-1-1

Figure 5.3. Part B—String Tetrachords

There also is melodic material that is unique to Part B. The long single note gesture in the cello described in chapter 3 appears only in Part B, and there is a cell in the piano that appears only in Part B (figures 2.9 and 5.4).[1] Clearly, the amount and variety of harmonic and pitch material in Part B in both the piano and the strings are greatly expanded in comparison to Part A. But it is texture that is the primary element shaping the structure of Part B.

Figure 5.4. Morton Feldman *Piano and String Quartet*
© Copyright 1985 by Universal Edition (London) Ltd., London / UE17972

STRUCTURE OF PART B (MM. 122–506)

Part B consists of three sections with durations of 1,184.5, 1,167, and 1,581 eighth notes, respectively. The total duration of Part B is 3,932.5 eighth notes, about five times that of Part A (see chapter 3, figure 3.5). The increased total duration in comparison to Part A is a function of the time and process required to achieve Part B's transformative purpose. As will be shown, the movement from the predominance of individual piano hexachords to the predominance of a specific pair of string tetrachords is done subtly, incrementally, and unhurriedly. But the greater duration is also a matter of scale, balancing the instability of Part B against the approximately equal duration of the stasis of Part C.[2]

Each section has characteristic material that makes it distinct. The differences in sonic character are somewhat interwoven, with seeds of an idea in one section coming to full bloom in a later section. However, it is the progression of change in the underlying sonic character of each section that drives the evolution of Part B and gives heft to its transformative purpose.

Section 1 (mm. 122–244)

The musical material that characterizes Section 1 consists of a succession of pairs of different piano chords. A single broken hexachord sonority, reminiscent of Part A, is sounded at the start of Part B (m. 122, figure 5.5).

Figure 5.5. Morton Feldman *Piano and String Quartet*
© Copyright 1985 by Universal Edition (London) Ltd., London / UE17972

This is followed almost immediately by the first pairing of hexachords (mm. 124–125, figure 5.5).

The sound of paired hexachords is reinforced a few measures later. Hexachord I^{t11} is followed by Hexachord V^{t1} and then repeated, locking the sound of paired hexachords in the listener's ear (figure 5.6).

Figure 5.6. Morton Feldman *Piano and String Quartet*
© Copyright 1985 by Universal Edition (London) Ltd., London / UE17972

In another few measures, a local manifestation of the large-scale purpose of Part B is presented: moving from hexachords to tetrachords (figure 5.7). A pair of repeated piano hexachords is followed by a pair of repeated pentachords, and finally, by a pair of repeated tetrachords. This progression from hexachords to tetrachords is clearly audible and quite apparent. Feldman could not be more explicit in conveying the transformative intent of Part B in this early passage, and in foreshadowing the paired tetrachords at the core of Part C.

Figure 5.7. Morton Feldman *Piano and String Quartet*
© Copyright 1985 by Universal Edition (London) Ltd., London / UE17972

These bars of Piano Alone textural material are followed by a series of shorter passages of Strings Alone, which likewise foreshadow Part C. The first such passage provides the initial appearance of tetrachord 2-1-2 in the

Detailed Analysis of Part B 73

Figure 5.8. Morton Feldman *Piano and String Quartet*
© Copyright 1985 by Universal Edition (London) Ltd., London / UE17972

strings in Part B (figure 5.8(a)). The importance of this moment is highlighted by the five repetitions and broken articulation of tetrachord 2-1-2 at this point. Two further instances of Strings Alone tetrachords, with multiple repetitions and broken articulation, occur soon after (figure 5.8(b–c)).

This leads, just three bars later, to the first appearance of the 1-2-1/2-1-2 tetrachord pair in the strings, sounded consecutively and repeated (figure 5.9).

Figure 5.9. Morton Feldman *Piano and String Quartet*
© Copyright 1985 by Universal Edition (London) Ltd., London / UE17972

The sounding of the 1-2-1/2-1-2 tetrachord pair in the strings occurs sporadically, in variable forms, throughout Part B. Here, the tetrachords are in reverse order and voiced differently from how they appear throughout Part C. But the salience of the four preceding string passages, together with the previous piano passage, is in how they illustrate the transformative function of Part B: from hexachords to tetrachords, from piano to strings, moving the composition unrelentingly toward Part C.

Section 2 (mm. 245–369)

In Section 2, the Piano Alone texture predominates once again. However, the aforementioned single note cell, employed in varying forms, replaces the chordal piano sonorities of Section 1 (see figure 5.4). This is followed by an exceptional moment in the composition: the strings imitating the piano cell (figure 5.10).³ This Antiphonal interplay between piano and strings foreshadows a similar imitative passage, discussed in Section 3, below.

Figure 5.10. Morton Feldman *Piano and String Quartet*
© Copyright 1985 by Universal Edition (London) Ltd., London / UE17972

The piano sonorities had been thinning from hexachords to tetrachords through Section 1. This process continues in Section 2 to a reduction to single notes. This prepares the listener for the shift from piano to strings in the foreground in Section 3.

Section 3 (mm. 370–506)

String tetrachords constitute the primary sonority of Section 3. What has been an incremental movement away from the piano as predominant across Sections 1 and 2 achieves its culmination at the very beginning of Section 3. The sound of Strings Alone broken tetrachords that were only hinted at in Section 1 become the center of attention from the start of Section 3; the instruments' overlapping sounding and release of notes adds a simulation of the sounding and decay of the piano (figure 5.11).

Figure 5.11. Morton Feldman *Piano and String Quartet*
© Copyright 1985 by Universal Edition (London) Ltd., London / UE17972

Two similar passages occur soon after (i.e., mm. 388–396 and mm. 418–432). In each of these three extended Strings Alone passages, the same repeated broken 2-1-1 tetrachord is voiced identically in the instruments, but with variability due to manipulations of meter. Not only has the predominant voice shifted from the piano to the strings, but also it is done as an echo of the repeated broken piano hexachords, decay, and metric manipulation that characterize Part A. Even more to the point, this 2-1-1 string tetrachord—with its pitches E3, A♭3, F♯4, and G5—draws from the pitches of and outlines piano Hexachord Ic, and has a similar form-consequential turning point impact as in Section 4 of Part A.

In between the second and third instance of these Strings Alone broken tetrachord passages, another remarkable passage is encountered (figure 5.12). This Antiphonal imitative passage is striking in how the strings

**Figure 5.12.   Morton Feldman *Piano and String Quartet* **
© Copyright 1985 by Universal Edition (London) Ltd., London / UE17972

exactly repeat the pitches and simulate the broken articulation and decay of the piano, with attention heightened somewhat by the pizzicato in the cello in m. 398. This implied sonic equivalence between strings and piano, coming amid the three extended passages of broken string tetrachords, further signals the evolution from piano to strings.

The ultimate target of this evolution first takes shape in mm. 456–58, where the 2-1-2/1-2-1 tetrachord progression is sounded first in the piano, and then in the strings (figure 5.13(a)). While the 2-1-2/1-2-1 string tetrachords have appeared throughout Part B, this is the first passage using similar pitches and voicing as in m. 509, the start of Part C (figure 5.13(b)).

The shift from the paired piano hexachords as the predominant sonority in Section 1 to the paired string tetrachords as predominant is clearly established in Section 3. This is all in preparation for, and as transition to, the paired string tetrachord sonorities at the heart of Part C.

**Figure 5.13.   Morton Feldman *Piano and String Quartet* **
© Copyright 1985 by Universal Edition (London) Ltd., London / UE17972

SUMMARY

Part B is sonically unstable in comparison to Part A. The amount of pitch/interval material in the piano and strings is greatly enlarged, the variety of harmonic activity is increased, and the use of transposed materials is expanded. Most of these materials are unique to Part B, some are carried over from Part A, and some foreshadow Part C.

The function of Part B is to move the composition from the sound of the single piano hexachords in Part A to the pairs of string tetrachords that dominate Part C, specifically the 2-1-2/1-2-1 tetrachord progression. This is achieved in three stages across the respective sections of Part B.

In Section 1, the density of the piano sonority decreases from hexachords to tetrachords. At the same time, the sounding of pairs of chordal structures is established. In Section 2, the density of the piano sonority decreases further, to a piano cell comprised of single notes. The imitation of this cell in the strings establishes the beginning of foreground equivalence between the piano and strings, a first step toward a shift in emphasis from piano to strings. Section 3 completes the transition to strings in the foreground. It begins with a single broken tetrachord—2-1-1—sounded in the Strings Alone texture and repeated numerous times. The 2-1-2/1-2-1 tetrachord progression appears sporadically in various guises throughout Part B in both the piano and strings, but toward the end of Section 3, is presented clearly in the strings in the voicing that characterizes Part C. These passages clearly complete the shift from piano to strings in the foreground. In essence, Part B constitutes a transformative process: hexachords to tetrachords, single sounds to pairs of sounds, piano to strings. Ultimately, it is the connective tissue that joins the stasis at the start of Part A to the stasis of Part C.

NOTES

1. Even though the notes are overlapping and the damper pedal is down, rather than being heard as broken trichords or tetrachords, the sonic character of this passage in the piano truly is one of a single note motive. This may be due in part to the large upward and downward interval skips of the variances of the motive, as well as to the contrast with the always upwardly rolled piano chords.

2. See chapter 1, note 45 and related quotation on page 11.

3. Compare especially m. 253 (figure 5.10) in the strings with m. 245 (figure 5.4) in the piano.

Chapter Six

Part C—Repetition, Variance, Stasis

Toward the end of his life, Feldman discussed the role of stasis as an important element in his conception of form.

> Penderecki said, there's only the sonata-allegro form. I say that the only form that I'm interested in is a kind of reversal of roles that were ordinarily historical. . . . For example, I like to take repetition and develop it, I like to take variation and make a stasis rather than continual variation, and repetition is stasis.[1]

The formal design of Part C is undergirded by this perspective. In fact, Feldman viewed the music in Part C as a "perfect example" of how repetition and variance[2] create stasis, and of how, together, they give form to his compositions.[3]

Stasis through repetition in Part C is exhibited foremost with respect to tetrachord content in the string parts. As noted in chapter 5, the strings are now in the foreground. Stasis arises from the repetition of the string tetrachord pair 2-1-2 (11, 1, 2, 4) and 1-2-1 (5, 6, 8, 9) for 290 of the 303 measures of Part C, sounding uninterrupted from mm. 519 to 806. Variance encountered throughout these tetrachord pair repetitions consists of inversions, shifts in register, and changes in meter and duration (table 6.1 and related figure 6.1(a) below).

The net aural effect of stasis is heightened through the repetition, for long stretches, of individual two-note cells in the first violin part. Generally, these two-note cells have the highest pitches of the respective tetrachord pairs. The most prominent of these are whole-step and perfect fourth cells. As such, each statement of a two-note cell is clearly audible, providing

Table 6.1. Tetrachords 2-1-2 and 1-2-1: Examples of Pitch, Register, and Meter Variances

	m. 519		m. 520		mm. 521–522	
	Meter	Pitch	Meter	Pitch	Meter	Pitch
Violin I	5/4	F♭5-G♭5	7/4	F♭5-G♭5	3/2+5/8	F♭5-G♭5
Violin II		D♭5-A♭4		C♭5-A♭4		D♭4-A♭3
Viola		C♭4-F3		D♭4-F3		D3-F3
Cello		D4-A2		D4-A2		B2-A2

a sonic "anchor" for the listener. Moreover, when a cell is periodically changed, that too is quite noticeable. Indeed, the occasional shift to different cells may be seen to mark sectional divisions within Part C (figure 6.1).

For example, the whole-step cell F♭5-G♭5 in Violin I begins in m. 519 and continues through m. 567, with a total of 88 repetitions, counting repeated bars. The B5-A5 whole-step cell first appears in mm. 568–576 for 14 repetitions. The perfect fourth cell—D♭6-A♭5—first appears in mm. 604–648 for 62 repetitions. These two-note cells in violin I, with extended repetitions, also return later in Part C. Together, these create a larger-scale overlay of repetitive activity that is at once recurring yet varied. It is this simultaneous aural experience of the local and the larger-scale repetition and variance that "keeps the music going"[4] and creates both a local and a larger-scale stasis from which—in Feldman's terms—form arises.

The F♭5-G♭5 cell is noteworthy in itself, not only for its pervasive presence throughout Part C, but for its reference back to Part A as well. It is a transposition of the F♯6-A♭6 whole-step cell that was prominently sounded throughout Part A in the highest octave of piano Hexachords I and II. Similarly, the B5-A5 cell in violin I is a transposition and inversion of that whole-step cell. Thus, the whole-step cell that was prominent in the piano in Part A is now switched to the strings in the new harmonic context of tetrachords 2-1-2 and 1-2-1 in Part C. This shift of the whole-step cell from the piano to the strings is consistent with a central thesis of this analysis: that the large-scale structure of the whole work moves from the predominance of the piano in Part A to the predominance of the strings in Part C.

In Part C, stasis in the piano arises in different ways than in the strings. Although there is a very wide range of chordal material in the piano, Hexachord X is the predominant repeating material (figure 6.2).

(a) Fb5-Gb5 Cell in Violin I

(b) B5-A5 Cell in Violin I

(c) Db6-Ab5 Cell in Violin I

Figure 6.1. Morton Feldman *Piano and String Quartet*
© Copyright 1985 by Universal Edition (London) Ltd., London / UE17972

Durations in 8th notes (Number of times sounded)		Pitch Content												Interval Content
		0	1	2	3	4	5	6	7	8	9	10	11	
		C	C#	D	D#	E	F	F#	G	G#	A	A#	B	
Hexachords															
X (Part B)	82 (4x)			D	D#	E	F				A	A#		1-1-1-4-1
	36 (2x)				D#	E	F	F#				A#	B	1-1-1-4-1^{T1}
	36 (2x)	C				E	F	F#	G				B	1-1-1-4-1^{T2}
	138 (7x)	C	C#				F	F#	G	G#				1-1-1-4-1^{T3}
	157 (8x)		C#	D				F#	G	G#	A			1-1-1-4-1^{T4}
1268 (63x)	122 (6x)			D	D#				G	G#	A	A#		1-1-1-4-1^{T5}
	128 (6x)				D#	E				G#	A	A#	B	1-1-1-4-1^{T6}
	158 (8x)	C				E	F				A	A#	B	1-1-1-4-1^{T7}
	123 (6x)	C	C#				F	F#				A#	B	1-1-1-4-1^{T8}
	124 (6x)	C	C#	D				F#	G				B	1-1-1-4-1^{T9}
	88 (4x)	C	C#	D	D#					G	G#			1-1-1-4-1^{T10}
	76 (4x)		C#	D	D#	E					G#	A		1-1-1-4-1^{T11}
XXIV	54 (3x)		C#			E		F#			A	A#	B	1-1-2-3-2
I (Part A/B)	190 (9x)			D	D#		F	F#	G		A			1-2-1-1-2^{T11}
XXV	42 (3x)	C	C#			E		F#			A		B	2-1-1-3-2
XXI (Part B)	28 (1x)	C				E			G		A	A#	B	3-2-1-1-1^{T11}
Septachord															
SEPTA-I	58 (4x)	C			D#		F			G#	A	A#	B	2-3-1-1-1-1
Pentachord															
PENT-VII	28 (2x)					E		F#		G#		A#	B	2-2-1-1
Tetrachords															
TET-III (B)	54 (2x)	C						F#	G	G#				1-1-4^{T7}
104 (4x)	50 (2x)	C				E						A#	B	1-1-4^{T11}
TET-XI	21 (1x)	C					F	F#	G					1-1-5
TET-IV (B)	16 (2x)						F	F#		G#	A			1-2-1
64 (4x)	32 (2x)							F#	G		A	A#		1-2-1^{T1}
	16 (2x)				D#	E		F#	G					1-2-1^{T10}
TET-XII	71 (6x)		C#							G#	A		B	1-2-2
TET-XIII	8 (1x)		C#	D				F#		G#				1-4-2
TET-VII (B)	30 (2x)		C#	D		E							B	2-1-2
84 (6x)	32 (2x)	C		D	D#		F							2-1-2^{T1}
	22 (2x)	C		D							A		B	2-1-2^{T10}
TET-XIV	21 (2x)					E				G#	A		B	4-1-2
Single Pitches															
	298 (22x)				D#									

Figure 6.2. Part C—Piano Chordal Structure and Single Pitches

Part C—Repetition, Variance, Stasis 83

Specifically, the piano presents Hexachord X exclusively from mm. 595–782, which comprises most of Part C.

In contrast to the homophonic tetrachord pairs in the strings, Hexachord X is broken. It sounds only intermittently, and for much less total duration than the strings, placing it in the background. Variance in the piano occurs through successive transpositions of Hexachord X without inversion, in contrast to the numerous inversions of the un-transposed string tetrachord pair, and shifts in register. While all 12 transpositions are sounded at least twice, they are never repeated immediately in succession, and may occur with varied durations between soundings (figure 6.3, figure 6.4). Finally, unlike the changing sets of long-repeated two-note cells in violin I that provide a sense of subsections to the overall structure, the successive transpositions of the piano hexachord are non-repeating and, thus, not in themselves form-defining in the same way.

Figure 6.3. Morton Feldman *Piano and String Quartet*
© Copyright 1985 by Universal Edition (London) Ltd., London / UE17972

Figure 6.4. Morton Feldman *Piano and String Quartet*
© Copyright 1985 by Universal Edition (London) Ltd., London / UE17972

The intermittent sounding of the piano against the continual sounding of the strings gives rise to the Antiphonal texture that permeates Part C. The sonic experience is of a familiar piano cell that recurs in answer to the strings, yet is subtly ever-changing. Together with the appearance in the strings of the whole-step piano cell from Part A now in a new harmonic and instrumental context in the strings in Part C, this local and large-scale repetition and variance may be the ultimate expression of what Feldman meant by "some things change while some things stay the same" in his sketches for *Piano and String Quartet*.[5]

THE STRUCTURE OF PART C—PALINDROMES

The overall form of Part C is comprised of introductory material, two overlapping palindromes of pitch/interval materials, one in the strings and one in the piano, and closing material (figure 6.5). The palindrome in the strings extends without interruption from mm. 572–806. The palindrome in the piano is in two parts separated by 20 measures of silence: mm. 595–674 and mm. 694–783.

Typically, a musical palindrome is a mirror image of musical material that is sounded and then reversed pitch-by-pitch: for example, C-E-F-G:G-F-E-C. However, in *Piano and String Quartet*, the units of statement and reversal are generally full measures of musical material rather than individual pitches. Thus, a sequence of measures is sounded and the material in those measures is later sounded with the sequence of matching measures being in reverse order. At times, there may be different or contrasting material in the center of the palindrome. For example, the material in measures 572–576 is reverse-ordered in mm. 806–802 (figure 6.6). The respective paired measures are mm. 572/806, 573/805, 574/804, 575/803, and 576/802. This retrograde pairing continues through mm. 682/694.[6] Although there are slight differences in the durations of the material in the matched measures, the inversions and voicings are, with few exceptions, identical (e.g., the viola part, comparing m. 572 and m. 806).

The palindrome in the piano is similar, with measure-to-measure pairings being the unit of statement and reverse ordering. These pairings hold with respect to pitch classes, intervals, and their order within measures, which match throughout the palindrome (although there are some instances where the register of these materials is different in the paired measure).

	Opening/First Section		Main Palindromes/Second Section		Closing
Piano	Introduction	Transition	Piano Palindrome < 1-1-1-4-1 (12 versions)	> Piano Palindrome 1-1-1-4-1 (12 versions)	
Measure	507–553	554–594	595–674	694–783	784–806 / 807–810
#Eighth-notes	914	653	1027	966	246 / 64

	Introduction and Transition			Over-arching String Palindrome 2-1-2 (11,1,2,4); 1-2-1 (5,6,8,9)			
Strings		Small String Palindrome *					
		559–571	572–585	572–648 < A	649–682 < B	683–693	694–723 > B'	724–806 > A'
Measure	507–558	216	236	1066	356	118	333	889
#Eighth-notes	1025							

*Small String Palindrome: MS. 559-585, overlaps with Over-arching String Palindrome: MS. 572–806.

Figure 6.5. Part C—Palindromes

86   Chapter Six

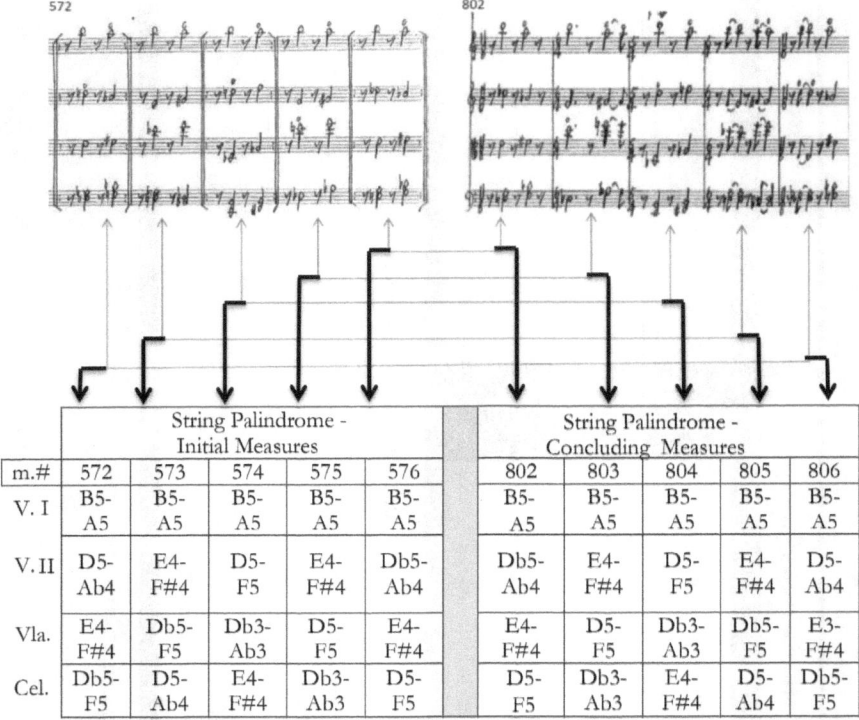

Figure 6.6. Over-arching String Palindrome Excerpts: Initial and Concluding Measures
Morton Feldman *Piano and String Quartet*
© Copyright 1985 by Universal Edition (London) Ltd., London / UE17972

The piano palindrome in Part C also provides instances of what Feldman has termed "crippled symmetry," in which there are subtle alterations in an otherwise symmetrical pattern. In the case of the piano palindrome, there are shifts in the reverse ordering of a few of the matched measures. Figure 6.7 displays an excerpt from the piano palindrome. The arrows show where the order of matched measures has shifted within the larger palindrome. For example, the order of mm. 601 and 603 is reversed in mm. 778 and 776. Similar shifts in ordering within the palindrome occur comparing mm. 607 and 609 with mm. 770 and 772, and also occur elsewhere in Part C.

Although the use of palindromic large-scale structure is unique to Part C, there are local instances of palindromes in *Piano and String Quartet*, which may be foreshadowing or preparatory. These local instances of palindromes occur in different ways.

Measure #	Transposition	Transposition	Measure #
(595)	(T⁰)*		
597	T^4	T^4	782
599	T^1	T^1	780
601	T^2	T^3	778
603	T^3	T^2	776
605	T^1	T^1	774
607	T^4	T^2	772
609	T^2	T^4	770
611	T^0	T^0	768
613	T^9	T^9	766
615	T^3	T^3	764
617	T^7	T^7	762
619	T^5	T^5	760
621	T^6	T^6	758

*The section of the music in which the piano palindrome appears begins with a hexachord that is not part of the palindrome.

Figure 6.7. Piano Palindrome by Measure and Transposition of Hexachord X—Excerpt

88 Chapter Six

A brief palindrome that is based on pitch, intervals, and the interplay between piano and strings occurs in Part B in mm. 138–144 (figure 6.8).

Figure 6.8. Morton Feldman *Piano and String Quartet*
© Copyright 1985 by Universal Edition (London) Ltd., London / UE17972

Feldman's palindromes can also be focused on time rather than on pitch, intervals, and/or instrumentation. These kinds of palindromes are based on meter and/or duration of sounds within bars. A palindrome that is structured by meter is found in Part B in mm. 460–468 (figure 6.9). The measure-to-measure matches are 460/468, 461/467, 462/466, and 463/465. Measure 464 is the center of the palindrome.

Figure 6.9. Morton Feldman *Piano and String Quartet*
© Copyright 1985 by Universal Edition (London) Ltd., London / UE17972

Another kind of palindrome is based on duration as well as meter (figure 6.10). Like those generally in this composition, the metric aspect of this palindrome is structured measure to measure. The meter is 7/4 in m. 509, 5/4 in m. 510, and 7/4 again in m. 511. In contrast, the durational aspect of this palindrome is structured by soundings within measures. This is evident comparing the duration of soundings in mm. 509 and 511. In m. 509 there are two soundings with duration of two beats and three beats, respectively, which is reversed in m. 511. The center of this palin-

Figure 6.10. Morton Feldman *Piano and String Quartet*
© Copyright 1985 by Universal Edition (London) Ltd., London / UE17972

drome, m. 510, has two soundings of equal value—1.5 beats each. Both the metric and durational palindromes exemplify crippled symmetry. The crippled symmetry arises in part from slight differences in the "matching" measures, but more saliently from the way the repeats are structured.

SUMMARY

The sonic character of Part C is stasis, with the strings in the foreground and piano in the background. This stasis arises predominantly from the single pair of tetrachords in the strings that is repeated and varied almost continually throughout Part C. Variances of the tetrachords occur through numerous inversions and alterations of duration, but never through transposition. Stasis in the piano comes from the use of a single hexachord as the predominant sound, varied primarily by transposition and register, but never by inversion. The intermittent sounding of this piano hexachord results in the Antiphonal texture that marks Part C. Formal divisions are experienced sonically in large part through the occurrence in violin I of several specific two-note cells in the highest register of the tetrachord pairs, which are repeated individually for many measures and then changed to another long-repeated cell. But on a deeper, more fundamental level, the sequence of varied tetrachord pairs and the separate sequence of piano hexachord transpositions form two overlapping palindromes that, along with introductory and closing material, constitute the overall large-scale structure of Part C.

NOTES

1. Feldman, Morton, ed. Raoul Mörchen, *Morton Feldman in Middelburg: Words on Music—Lectures and Conversations, Vol. 1* (Köln: Ed. MusikTexte, 2008) 338.

2. Feldman uses the term "variation" in the quote, but since he does not mean this term in the classical sense of theme and variation, the term "variance" is being used instead in this text. See also chapter 4, notes 12 and 13.

3. Feldman, Morton, *Morton Feldman in Middelburg*, 338.

4. Feldman had said that the problem he had to solve with the late long works was "how to keep them going."

Feldman, Morton, *Morton Feldman in Middelburg*, 124, 198, 604 (*Vol. 2*), also chapter 1, note 15 and related text on page 3.

5. See appendix E.

6. The material in mm. 683–693 consists of the same 2-1-2/1-2-1 tetrachords, but the ordering is not palindromic.

Chapter Seven

Conclusion—The Sonic Experience of *Piano and String Quartet*

Morton Feldman, a brilliant, intrepid, and encyclopedic analyst of great music himself, viewed the idea of academicians analyzing his scores with some reservation. But in particular, he viewed it as an insufficient means of experiencing his compositions.

> Don't ever write an article on my music! Because you only could approximate it . . . you could get close, but we're too prejudiced, one way or the other. . . . Just do a statistical analysis. Very cut and dry. And leave out the conclusion. No synthesis, just give the information.[1]

> So I like to formulate what the piece needs even in terms of its plasticity, in terms of silence, form . . . and you don't hear it, you don't hear it! That is, you don't hear what you see [in the score].[2]

This author confesses to having taken Feldman's admonitions to heart. Not that analysis of his music is futile; only that analysis is by its nature limited and incomplete. No matter how extensive the effort, it will not be exhaustive. Necessarily, some aspect of the music will be left out, whether through avoidance of overabundance of detail or through oversight. Recognizing their validity, the author found these admonitions a source of apprehension and humility, to be used with care as a guide in the somewhat daunting task of describing the music that is the subject of this book. That task, then, was purposely limited to answering the two key questions set out in the introduction: first, What keeps the music going? and second, What is it about *Piano and String Quartet* that embodies the achievement of "everything that Feldman wanted"?

The analyses in chapters 3 through 6 attempt to address the first question, focusing on the materials and structure of *Piano and String Quartet*. The analyses describe the work's pitch and chordal structures; use of texture; the foreground/background predominance of the instruments; the treatment of meter and duration; the various forms of manipulation of these elements; the control of stasis and instability through the interplay of repetition, variance, and juxtaposition of musical materials; and how a recognizable structure emerges from examining all of these factors. Perhaps this description is what Feldman meant by a "cut and dry . . . statistical analysis." But they are clearly the primary elements that "keep the music going."

Whether the analysis is at the micro level (i.e., the designation of specific materials), at the mid-level (i.e., the designation of sections and subsections), or at the macro level (i.e., the description of the movement from stasis to instability to stasis), what we have depicts in words and images the surface of the music. This depiction is drawn from a close examination of the score. And as Feldman states, "You don't hear what you see." In other words, examining his scores is not the equivalent of the sonic experience of his music. He might even say that the notation is a far cry from the aural experience, and thus woefully inadequate as a representation of his composition.

Clearly, it was the sound itself—and its experience—that concerned Feldman. He had an inescapable drive to create a sound world that was truly new, envisioning what he called "a totally abstract sonic adventure."[3] Consequently, addressing the second but most fundamental question posed in the introduction—What is it about this particular work that embodies the achievement of "everything that Feldman wanted"?—requires a review of his overriding aesthetic goals in light of the sonic experience of *Piano and String Quartet*.

As noted previously, Feldman's lifelong dedication was to compose music that was independent of the forms, practices, processes, and sounds that had come before—what he referred to as the yoke of music history. This intention undergirded his experiments in the early 1960s to free pitch, duration, meter, and timbre using new forms of notation, the return to precise notation in the 1970s "to control the silence," and his revelations about scale in his late period. At its most fundamental, his desire was "not to 'compose,' but to project sounds into time, free from a compositional rhetoric."[4] By 1965, Feldman had refined his thinking about the meaning of "projecting sounds into time."

> Change is the only solution to an unchanging aural plane created by the constant element of projection of attack. This is perhaps why in my own music I am so involved with the decay of each sound and try to make its attack sourceless. The attack of a sound is not its character. Actually, what we hear is the attack and not the sound. Decay, however, this departing landscape, *this* expresses where the sound exists in our hearing—leaving us, rather than coming toward us.[5]

The interplay among attack (i.e., "sounding" as used herein), sustain, and decay appears in Feldman's music throughout his career. However, in *Piano and String Quartet*, these sonic characteristics become the explicit focal point, assuming center stage as the fundamental underlying organizing principle of this composition. The evidence for this assertion is found in the opening measure and validated through attentive listening of the complete work. That the content of the opening measure is salient—and foundational—to the rest of the piece is based on Feldman's description of his approach to composing, made during a lecture on August 2, 1983, two years before *Piano and String Quartet* was completed.

> I don't even have a word like "process" in my thinking, but strategy, and a strategy usually comes about in terms of the same kind of thinking that any other composer would have. Like anybody else, the opening measure and its potential and its flexibility. But what I don't do is try to make a system out of it.[6]

In this case, because of the consistent pairing of alternating sounding/decaying measures that appear throughout Part A, the "opening measure" is in actuality mm. 1–2 in the score. These two measures not only present the material whose "potential and flexibility" will be exercised by the composer, but they also exemplify Feldman's lament that "you don't hear what you see" in the notation. This discrepancy between notation and sound can be seen by comparing the score of mm. 1–2 with a spectrograph of the same measures (figure 7.1). While a spectrograph is not a substitute for the experience of the "acoustical reality" that comes from listening to a piece of music, it does go some distance in addressing Feldman's lament

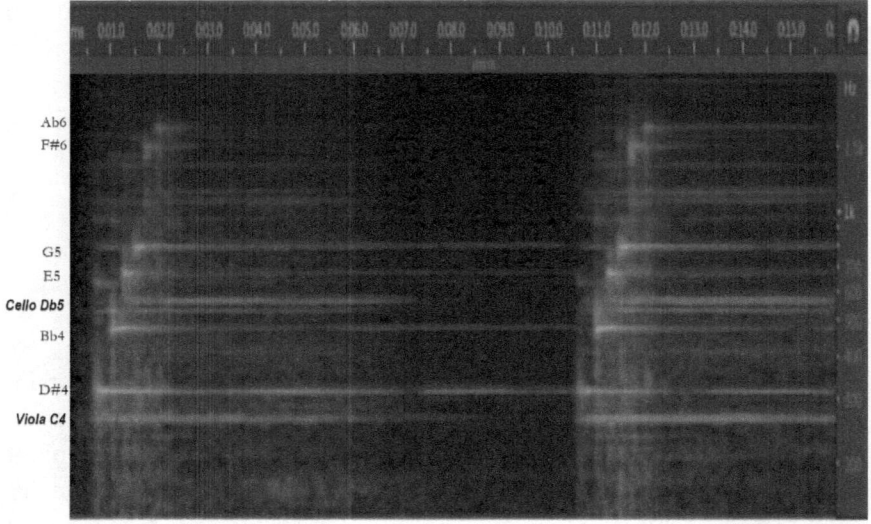

Figure 7.1. Spectrograph and Score, Measures 1–3, *Piano and String Quartet*
© Copyright 1985 by Universal Edition (London) Ltd., London / UE17972

by providing an objective representation of the sounds produced, as opposed to what is notated.

The score indicates a dynamic of pianississimo, muted strings, and the damper pedal down throughout, but no tempo marking.[7] It displays musical material being sounded and sustained in m. 1 in the piano, viola, and cello, and only an indication of meter change in m. 2, with no sounded musical material notated in what otherwise is an empty bar. Of course, that empty bar is not devoid of sound despite the fact that there are no ties or notes indicated. The spectrograph plainly displays the release of the strings just before m. 2 and the decay of the sounds of the piano through the end of m. 2. It also shows how the length of decay in the piano is associated with register: the first four notes of the piano hexachord (in register 4 and 5) decay through the end of m. 2, while the decay of the F#6-A♭6 cell ends about a third of the way through the first bar.

While the broken hexachord in the piano and the pitches in the viola and cello provide the surface of the music, it is my belief that the opposition of release in the strings and decay in the piano constitute its core. This opposition is presented over and again in similar fashion—that is, with the same piano hexachord (subtly varied) and slightly varying pitch combinations in the strings—15 consecutive times over mm. 1–30 (i.e., through all of Section 1 of Part A). The opposition of release and decay is explicit, the purposeful changes in meter in the alternating measures put a spotlight on the decay of the piano, and the many repetitions make recognition of the aural presence of release and decay almost unavoidable. Further, within the piano hexachord, there is a kind of internal opposition in the release in m. 1 of the two pitches in the highest register and the decay in m. 2 of the remaining four pitches in the lower two registers. Finally, the slow tempo and very soft dynamics provide the listener the sonic space and time needed for awareness to this opposition to arise.

The opposition of release and decay, I would say, is the raw, most basic material upon which *Piano and String Quartet* is built. It is present in every measure of the composition, with its "potential and flexibility" realized in manifold ways by Feldman, but exploited somewhat differently in each of the three respective parts of the composition described in the preceding chapters. These different ways to exploit the opposition of release and decay correlate with the changes in texture and instrument in the foreground that define the structure. Thus, as the composition moves through its respective parts, there is an evolution in the nature of the opposition, with decay in the piano having predominance in Part A, this predominance moving from decay in the piano to release in the strings over the course of Part B, and release in the strings having predominance in Part C.

96   Chapter Seven

Measures 1 and 2 exemplify the predominance of the decay in the piano relative to the release in the strings that is present throughout Part A (see figure 7.1 above). Part B begins with a continuation of the piano decay as predominant, but the repeated release of the same string tetrachord—highlighted by rests—along with the dovetail texture, begins the change in the balance of opposition between decay and release (figure 7.2). This serves as a signal of the significant change to come.

Figure 7.2. Morton Feldman *Piano and String Quartet*
© Copyright 1985 by Universal Edition (London) Ltd., London / UE17972

The closing measures of Part B confirm the change that has evolved (figure 7.3). Here the piano decay is much thinner—now a repeated intervallic cell rather than the fully rolled broken hexachord found at the

Figure 7.3. Morton Feldman *Piano and String Quartet*
© Copyright 1985 by Universal Edition (London) Ltd., London / UE17972

beginning of Part B—and sounded separate and apart from the strings. The sonic experience of the release of the strings is clearly spotlighted by the nine repetitions of tetrachords and their being sounded without the intermingling of the piano decay.

The contrast between Part A and the end of Part B could not be made plainer. The predominance of the sonic opposition has moved from piano decay to string release, all in preparation for Part C, in which release in the strings predominates. This is illustrated most directly in a passage that begins the closing of Part C (figure 7.4).

Figure 7.4. Morton Feldman *Piano and String Quartet*
© Copyright 1985 by Universal Edition (London) Ltd., London / UE17972

The sense of release in the strings is heightened by the rests—the silence—that separate what are now pairs of the same two tetrachords, which are sounded in every measure. The sounding of the piano in Part C does not occur in every measure; it is intermittent. Their many fewer occurrences are also lesser in weight. Even though its notes are in the shape of a broken hexachord, there is much less sustain and decay in this dotted-eighth figure than in the typical rolled hexachords of Part A. Accordingly, Part C is marked by a considerable reduction in sustain and decay in the piano and an increase in the sonic experience of release in the strings, in comparison to Part A.

In summary, the sonic experience of *Piano and String Quartet* is grounded in the opposition of decay in the piano and release in the strings. Over its course, the work evolves from decay in the piano as predominant to release in the strings as predominant. The form of the composition is immanent in this opposition; it emerges solely from Feldman's exploitation of this opposition, working with the "potential and flexibility" of the surface material.

Arnold Schoenberg said, "The unity of musical space demands an absolute and unitary perception."[8] There is an absolute and unitary perception that pervades *Piano and String Quartet*: the sonic opposition of decay and release. No other work of Feldman's employs the opposition of decay and release with the clarity, dexterity, and wit as *Piano and String Quartet*. No other work of his brings to light the "departing [sonic] landscape" he sought throughout his career with the eloquence and focus of *Piano and String Quartet*. Without doubt, its composition represents the apotheosis of freedom from the yoke of history. Indeed, *Piano and String Quartet was* everything Morton Feldman ever wanted.

NOTES

1. Feldman, Morton, ed. Raoul Mörchen, *Morton Feldman in Middelburg: Words on Music—Lectures and Conversations, Vol. 1* (Köln: Ed. MusikTexte, 2008), 132.

2. Ibid., 222.

3. Feldman, Morton, ed. B. H. Friedman, *Give My Regards to Eighth Street*, (Cambridge: Exact Exchange 2002), 6.

4. Feldman, Morton, Liner notes, "Feldman, Brown," Time Records No. 58007, 1963, New York.

5. "The Anxiety of Art," Feldman, Morton, *Essays*, Walter Zimmerman, editor (Kerpen: Beginner Press, 1985), in Thomas DeLio, *The Music of Morton Feldman* (Westport, CT/London: Greenwood Press, 1996), 207.

6. "Johannesburg Lecture, 2 August 1983," in Chris Villars, *Morton Feldman Says* (London: Hyphen Press, 2006), 176.

7. See chapter 2, note 7, for a discussion of the tempo of *Piano and String Quartet*.

8. Schoenberg, Arnold, *Style and Idea* (New York: Philosophical Library, 1950), 113.

Appendix A
Key for Locating Measures in the Score of Piano and String Quartet

Each page of the score is numbered and has three systems, each with nine measures. The table below provides the page number of the score and the measure number of the first measure of each successive system.

Piano and String Quartet Score

Page number	System	First measure number
1	First	1
	Second	10
	Third	19
2	First	28
	Second	37
	Third	46
3	First	55
	Second	64
	Third	73
4	First	82
	Second	91
	Third	100
5	First	109
	Second	118
	Third	127
6	First	136
	Second	145
	Third	154

Appendix A

Page number	System	First measure number
7	First	163
	Second	172
	Third	181
8	First	190
	Second	199
	Third	208
9	First	217
	Second	226
	Third	235
10	First	244
	Second	253
	Third	262
11	First	271
	Second	280
	Third	289
12	First	298
	Second	307
	Third	316
13	First	325
	Second	334
	Third	343
14	First	352
	Second	361
	Third	370
15	First	379
	Second	388
	Third	397
16	First	406
	Second	415
	Third	424

Key for Locating Measures in the Score of Piano and String Quartet

Page number	System	First measure number
17	First	433
	Second	442
	Third	451
18	First	460
	Second	469
	Third	478
19	First	487
	Second	496
	Third	505
20	First	514
	Second	523
	Third	532
21	First	541
	Second	550
	Third	559
22	First	568
	Second	577
	Third	586
23	First	595
	Second	604
	Third	613
24	First	622
	Second	631
	Third	640
25	First	649
	Second	658
	Third	667
26	First	676
	Second	685
	Third	694

Appendix A

Page number	System	First measure number
27	First	703
	Second	712
	Third	721
28	First	730
	Second	739
	Third	748
29	First	757
	Second	766
	Third	775
30	First	784
	Second	793
	Third	802

Appendix B

Photocopy of Letter from Morton Feldman to Aki Takahashi, Most Likely September 11, 1985

> Sept 11
>
> Dear Aki,
>
> Never expected to write a piece with just broken chords! We're in Paris (saw Beckett) and you would have a concert there in mid June — but — your new schedule rules it out. Next year. So let's plan to leave

Figure App B.1.

Appendix C
Selected Bibliography: Analytical Studies of the Music of Morton Feldman

Early Period: 1950–1969	
Title of Work	Analysis: Author and Bibliographic Information
Projection 1 (1950)	Welsh, John P. "Projection I (1950)." In DeLio, Thomas, ed., *The Music of Morton Feldman*. Westport, CT: Greenwood Press (1996), 21–38
Nature Pieces for Piano (1951)	Ender, Daniel. "Impressionen zwischen den Zeilen: Einige abschweifende Überlegungen zu den Nature Pieces von Morton Feldman." *Neue Zeitschrift für Musik* (1991–), Vol. 173, No. 1, MUSIK	NATUR (2012), 38–43
Intermission 5 (1952) Piano Piece (1952) Intermission 6 (1953) Intersection 3 (1953) Intermission 6 (1953)	Noble, Alastair. *Composing Ambiguity: The Early Music of Morton Feldman*. Surry, England: Ashgate Publishing Limited (2013) Ortiz de Zarate, Juan. "Intermission VI (Morton Feldman)." *Música e investigación: Revista del Instituto Nacional de Musicología 'Carlos Vega'*, 7(14–15) (2004), 81–92
Projection 1–5, Intersection 1–4, Marginal Intersection, The King of Denmark, Atlantis, The Straits of Magellan, Ixion, Out of last pieces, In Search of an Orchestration	Cline, David. "Allover Method and Holism in Morton Feldman's Graphs." *Perspectives of New Music*, Vol. 51, No. 1 (Winter 2013), 56–98 Also see: Cline, David. *The Graph Music of Morton Feldman*. Cambridge: Cambridge University Press (2016)
Projection 4 (1951)	Vigil, Ryan. "'Projection 4' and an Analytical Methodology for Morton Feldman's Graphic Works." *Perspectives of New Music*, Vol. 47, No. 1 (Winter 2009), 233–267

Title of Work	Analysis: Author and Bibliographic Information
Piano (Three Hands) (1957)	Corrado, Omar. "*Piano (Three Hands)* De Morton Feldman Un Analisis Y Sus Contornos." *Pauta*, Vol. 12, No. 45 (1993), 64–73
Last Pieces #3 (1959)	DeLio, Thomas. "Last Pieces #3 (1959)." In DeLio, Thomas, ed., *The Music of Morton Feldman*. Westport, CT: Greenwood Press (1996), 39–70
Durations 3 (1961)	DeLio, Thomas. "Toward an Art of Imminence: Morton Feldman's *Durations 3*." In DeLio, Thomas, *Analytical Studies of the Music of Ashley, Cage, Carter, Dallapiccola, Feldman, Lucier, Reich, Satie, Schoenberg, Wolff, and Xenakis: Essays in Contemporary Music*. Lewiston, NY: Edwin Mellen Press (2017)
Rabbi Akiba (1963)	Levy, Benjamin R. "Vertical Thoughts: Feldman, Judaism, and the Open Aesthetic," *Contemporary Music Review*, 32:6 (2013), 571–588
The King of Denmark (1964)	Welsh, John P. "The Secret Structure in Morton Feldman's The King of Denmark (1964) Part One." *Percussive Notes, Journal of the Percussive Arts Society*, Vol. 46, No. 2 (April 2008), 34–40 Welsh, John P. "The Secret Structure in Morton Feldman's The King of Denmark (1964) Part Two." *Percussive Notes, Journal of the Percussive Arts Society*, Vol. 46, No. 3 (June 2008), 32–39
Piano Piece 1952 (1964)	Wolff, Christian. *Occasional Pieces: Writings and Interviews*, 1952–2013. New York: Oxford University Press (2017), 99–103

Selected Bibliography: Analytical Studies of the Music of Morton Feldman   107

Middle Period: 1969–1977

Title of Work	Analysis: Author and Bibliographic Information
The Viola In My Life (1) (1970)	DeLio, Thomas. "The Marvelous Illusion: Morton Feldman's The Viola In My Life (1) (1970)." Contemporary Music Review, Vol. 32, No. 6 (2013), 589–638 Wiener, Oliver. Morton Feldman, "The Viola in My Life (1970–71)." Saarbrucken: Pfau (Fragment; H. 11), 1996
I met Heine on the Rue Furstenberg (1971)	Thomas, Margaret. "The 'Departing Landscape': Temporal and Timbral Elasticity in Morton Feldman's I met Heine on the Rue Furstenberg." Ex tempore, Analytical and Theoretical Papers from the Department of Music, the University of California at San Diego. Vol. 11 No. 1 (2002), 73–86
Three Clarinets, Cello, and Piano (1971)	Hamman, Michael. "Three Clarinets, Cello, and Piano (1971)." In DeLio, Thomas, ed. The Music of Morton Feldman. Westport, CT: Greenwood Press (1996), 71–98
Rothko Chapel (1971)	Johnson, Steven. "Rothko Chapel and Rothko's Chapel." Perspectives of New Music, Vol. 32, No. 2 (Summer, 1994), 6–53 Lanza, Mauro. "Per Una Segmentazione di Rothko Chapel di Morton Feldman." Musica e storia, VIII/1 (2000), 127–143
Instruments I (1974)	Böttinger, Peter. "Das exakt Ungefahre: Ein analytischer Versuch über Instruments I (1974) von Morton Feldman." In Morton Feldman, München: Edition Text + Kritik, [1986], 105–114

Late Period: 1977–1986

Title of Work	Analysis: Author and Bibliographic Information
Spring of Chosroes (1977)	Paynter, Terrence. "Form and Process in Morton Feldman's *Spring of Chosroes.*" *Music Analysis*, Vol. 34, No. 1 (2015), 47–90
Piano (1977)	Ames, Paula Kopstick. "Piano (1977)." In DeLio, Thomas, ed., *The Music of Morton Feldman*. Westport, CT: Greenwood Press (1996), 99–146
Why Patterns (1978)	Johnson, Steven. "Jasper Johns and Morton Feldman: What Patterns?" In Johnson, Steven, ed., *The New York Schools of Music and Visual Arts*. New York: Routledge (2002), 217–247 Timonova, Arina Al. "The Idea and Its Realization in Morton Feldman's Piece 'Why Patterns?'" *Muzykovedenie*, No 7. (2013), 35–45
Patterns in a Chromatic Field (Untitled Composition) (1981)	Hummel, Thomas. "Qualitativer Sprung: Morton Feldmans Untitled Composition."*Musiktexte* 52 (1994), 51–56
Triadic Memories (1981)	Egli, Urs. " Les souffrances d'un interprète (sérieux): Triadic memories (1981) de Morton Feldman." *Dissonanz/Dissonance* 80 (2003), 12–21 Jurkowski, Edward. "Harmonic and Formal Coherence in Morton Feldman's Late Music." In *Beyond the Centres: Musical Avant Gardes since 1950: In Memoriam Yannis Andreou Papaioannou* (1910–1989), 2010 Johnson, Steven. "It Must Mean Something: Narrative in Beckett's *Molloy* and Feldman's *Triadic Memories.*" *Contemporary Music Review*, Vol. 32, No. 6 (2013), 639–668
Bass Clarinet and Percussion (1981)	Etkin, Mariano. "Un 'error' en Bass clarinet and percussion de Morton Feldman." *Revista del Instituto Superior deMusica*, U.N.L., Vol. 10 (2005), 56–61
For John Cage (1982)	York, Wes. "For John Cage (1982)." In DeLio, Thomas, ed. *The Music of Morton Feldman*. Westport, CT: Greenwood Press (1996), 147–198
Three Voices (1982)	McGuire, John, "Wiederholung und Veränderung: Morton Feldmans Three Voices." *Musiktexte* 20 (1987) 26–29
String Quartet II (1983)	Wolff, Christian. *Occasional Pieces: Writings and Interviews, 1952–2013*. New York: Oxford University Press (2017) 229–234

Selected Bibliography: Analytical Studies of the Music of Morton Feldman

Title of Work	Analysis: Author and Bibliographic Information
Crippled Symmetry (1983)	Hanninen, Dora A. "A Theory of Recontextualization in Music: Analyzing Phenomenal Transformations of Repetition." *Music Theory Spectrum*, Vol. 25, No. 1 (Spring 2003), 59–97
For Bunita Marcus (1985)	Franke, Daniel. "Analytische Contemplation des Feldmanschen Klavierstückes 'For Bunita Marcus.'" In *Morton Feldman*, München: Edition Text + Kritik (1986), 135–147
Coptic Light (1985)	Karallus, Manfred. "Resistance gegen die Welt: Morton Feldmans 'Coptic Light.'" *Musiktexte* 52 (1994), 47–50 Hanninen, Dora A. "Feldman, Analysis, Experience." *Twentieth-Century Music*, Vol. 1, No. 2 (2004), 225–251
Palais de Mari (1986)	Mörchen, Raoul. "Music as a Musical Process: Morton Feldmans Palais de Mari." *Musiktexte* 66 (1996), 53–62 Hanninen, Dora A. *A Theory Of Music Analysis: On Segmentation and Associative Organization*. Rochester: University of Rochester (2012), 331–359
Piano, Violin, Viola, Cello (1987)	Hanninen, Dora A. "Feldman, Analysis, Experience." *Twentieth-century Music*, Vol. 1, No. 2 (2004), 225–251

Appendix D
Interview with David Harrington (excerpted): Morton Feldman's Piano and String Quartet

David Harrington is the first violinist with the Kronos Quartet. The Kronos Quartet had a long association with composer Morton Feldman and premiered his works for string quartet. Along with pianist Aki Takahashi, the Kronos Quartet premiered Feldman's *Piano and String Quartet* on November 2, 1985, at the New Music America Festival in Los Angeles and recorded it in November 1991. Mr. Harrington was interviewed by telephone on March 28, 2017 (Part I), and April 11, 2017 (Part II).

PART I

David Harrington: Here's the story of how [Morton Feldman's] *Piano and String Quartet* originated. We were in . . . I believe it was Toronto . . . performing [Feldman's] *String Quartet II* . . . and this would have probably been, I think in 1982.¹ And the CBC, the Canadian Broadcasting Company, was recording *String Quartet II*. They were doing a one-hour delayed broadcast.

The concert started at 7 p.m. and we had to be done right at the stroke of 11 p.m., so that they could rebroadcast the concert from 8 to 12 p.m. And at 12 midnight, the Canadian national anthem came on unfailingly every night of the year. And that is how *String Quartet II* became the four-hour quartet: Kronos had to do a fast tempo to fit that piece into four hours.²

We had played Morton's *Structures*. . . . We had played all of his works for string quartet up to that point, including *String Quartet I*.

He was not shy, and loved applause, and he loved relating to audiences. And usually, he'd give some kind of speech. I mean, after we gave *String Quartet I*, he gave a speech about the piece. He silenced the applause and did that.

And so we finished *String Quartet II* [having played it straight through for four hours without a break]. We were completely exhausted. We stood up; there was wonderful applause. I motioned to Morton and I thought for sure he would get up and come up on stage. Well, he didn't. And we were concerned—that there was something wrong with our performance, or something.

And later, at the party, after the concert—and by then the delayed broadcast was on, so that at the party you were hearing *String Quartet II* as well. I went over to Morton and said, "Morton, is everything OK with our performance?" And he said, "Oh, yes!" He was very complimentary.

And I said, "Well, how come you didn't come up on stage and take a bow?" And he looked at me and said, "David, I had to take a pee so bad, I was afraid I wouldn't make it."

And I said, "Morton, maybe the next piece you write for Kronos should be shorter." And the next piece he wrote, and the final piece he wrote for Kronos, was *Piano and String Quartet*, for us and Aki Takahashi. And that is why it is not four or more hours long.

Ray Fields: That's right—79 minutes. I did wonder, how do the musicians manage all that playing time without a break?

DH: Well, it's physically, immensely challenging. And in fact, we were going to do it one more time. Kronos has probably done it—*String Quartet II*—more than anyone else, and there have been performances where they do an hour at a time and then take a break and then do another hour—and you know, we always did it all the way through—and we did it a total of eight times.

We were going to do it one more time in New York. We thought we would "take it home" to New York, many years after we had done it initially. We started rehearsing and several of us got incredible shooting pains in our limbs during rehearsal. It was the only time we've ever had to cancel something—cancel a performance. And Morton would have been kind of pleased in a certain way, because we got more publicity for a concert we didn't play. He was sort of into publicity, being larger than life.

You know, it is a very, very difficult thing to do, and you have to work toward the length of those pieces. You need to practice, spending 20 minutes at a time and then add to it and then add to that. You know, it is really tough.

And to play soft requires so much more strength than to play loud. And people don't realize that sometimes, but it does.

RF: I've wondered how stressful it is for the musicians. And I've thought even about *Piano and String Quartet*, it's so wonderful to listen to, but how does it feel to play it?

DH: Well, it's magical actually. And you go through—even on *Piano and String Quartet*, which is so much shorter than *String Quartet II*, for example—even on that piece you go through major physical issues, of certain pain. It's tough to do. But there's something that always happens in Morton's music, the longer pieces. The music and the incredible beauty of it takes over. And it is highly advisable—I really recommend players trying to play his pieces, the long pieces—it is really amazing—and you go into a zone that you never thought existed before.

RF: That's a great story and it is recorded. Thank you.

PART II

Mr. Harrington is in the Kronos Library, looking at the copies of the score the Kronos Quartet used for the premiere and recording of *Piano and String Quartet*, to address questions about the score and to see whether there are any notes about Morton Feldman's intentions, directions, or corrections.

Ray Fields: Do you have the score as well as the individual parts?

David Harrington: We played off of the score—[you and I] are looking at the same thing.[3] I have absolutely no information from him [written on the score used for the first violin]. Usually I would write things that the composer said. Let me see if anybody else did. Not seeing anything in the second violin part either—checking the viola part—

Did you say you were going to contact Aki Takahashi? I think contacting her would be a great thing to do. She and Morton were very close—not seeing anything [on the viola part]. Usually we would write things in our parts that the composer would say. So I'm now on the cello part—

RF: So there are no notes anywhere? I found a couple of things that I thought were a little ambiguous. You obviously, from the recording, decided how to resolve those ambiguities, but I wondered if the parts were marked up.

DH: Well, tell me the ambiguities and I'll—

RF: Okay. On page 18, just as an example, in the first system, the second violin, do you see that A flat?

DH: Yeah.

RF: So that A flat carries across [several measures by ties]. And he was very, very meticulous about his notation. But when you get to the fifth measure, that A on the 4th and 5th beats is not indicated with a flat, but you do play it with a flat on the recording.

DH: And how about the viola part?

RF: And the same thing with the viola part. It is played as a C sharp [where the pitch C is carried across measures by ties but the sharp sign is not present].

DH: Yep. That's interesting. Now, at this point in the history of Kronos, that would have been changed—in our parts that we played from. I'm absolutely certain that we asked Morton about that and it was—that we did exactly what he—what was recorded is what was played for him in rehearsal. Definitely. There is not even a question about that. The thing is, what we played in concert and on the recording would have been what he heard in rehearsal, definitely, even though the score looks the way it looks.

RF: Right. I was only wondering if you had marked that up, or if anyone had.

DH: It should have been, and like I say, now it would have been, and I'm kind of surprised that John and Hank did not do that, I have to say. Is there anything in the first violin part—it would be interesting to see, because I'm usually very meticulous about that kind of thing.

RF: No, I don't see anything in the first violin part. There are one or two in the piano. I played along with those on my keyboard as Aki played it [on the recording] and so I was able to resolve them. Some of the gestures are transpositions, and there are one or two places where it looked like there was a notational mistake, and she played them the way they would have been transposed.[4]

No, I don't see anything in the first violin part that I have a question about, other than enharmonics. What I wondered was—in what I consider the third section, the last section, has, for example, F flat 5-G flat 5 wherever it appears in the first violin and E 4-F sharp 4 in the cello. What I see as a B in one voice may appear as a C flat in another voice. What I have wondered is whether you would have played those differently?

DH: We've always been mystified by that aspect of Morton's writing. In the *String Quartet II*, he does double-flats and things like that, where you will be playing along and there will be an F flat, or I can't remember the exact pitch, but it was very, very confusing what he actually meant. And we ended up thinking that it was slightly color—coloring, so that he actually did mean a slightly different pitch. Can you tell me which bar you are talking about?

RF: On page 20, if you look at the second system, you have F flat–G flat. Then on page 23, in the first system, second measure and fourth measure, and these are ostensibly the same chords, you have E-F sharp in the second violin part. That's just an example. Other examples—as you see above, the first violin is playing B5. In the second system, second violin, second measure, you have C flat 4. Would you have talked about that?

DH: The thing is, when we're playing with a piano, we would tune it to the piano, if we're playing together. So there would be very, very slight fluctuations of intonation. What would sound in tune to us—and it would depend—it is so hard to describe this because you almost do it intuitively. I think the safest thing to say is we would play piano intonation, so that it is slightly tempered, no matter what he wrote.

RF: So a C flat and a B, and an F flat and an E, would be pretty much the same.

DH: They would be, yes, unless the chord suggested something else—and if the piano were not playing. So for example, if we were tuning an E natural to the open C-string of the cello and the piano were not playing, we would play the E low. But if the piano were playing the C and the E, we would have to tune the C and the E to the piano.

RF: Very often, the piano and the strings are in different chromatic fields in this piece. There are places where there is overlap. But here in the third section, where this gesture in the piano is continually being transposed, there will be notes that are shared and notes that are not.

DH: I do not have an explanation for why Morton did that [speaking of the enharmonics in the strings].

RF: But was it something you discussed with him?

DH: I am thinking back to the *String Quartet II*, because there were things in that that were even more dramatic—in terms of the notation. And, as I recall, he said something about the coloring, and then he described his fascination with Turkish rugs. And he described the dipping of thread into ink, and how the thread would be saturated with color in various ways, and how fascinating it was to look at these handmade rugs and hand-colored threads of the rugs. And so that provided a kind of overall sense of his idea of intonation—kind of the reason for an F flat as opposed to an E natural—or an F double-flat instead of an Eb.

RF: And leaving it to the musician to—get it on that right cent.

DH: Yes. The last time I asked Morton about *String Quartet II*, because what I noticed, if you look really carefully at the notation, his notation seems to change. And I asked him about that. And that is from day to day. He would compose so many measures a day, and then the next day or the next week, whenever he came back to that piece, his notation was slightly different. That may be part of what we're seeing here, in the notation. He may have actually changed the enharmonics depending on when he was composing or what day it was.

RF: When it appears in the first violin it is always F flat5-G flat5, and always B5-A5 in that upper voice. So that's very consistent throughout this last section. These differences [in enharmonics] show up in the other voices.

About the carpets—in my reading about him and in his interviews, he talks about Philip Guston and Jasper Johns, and how elements of their art prompted his thinking about a musical problem. So I wondered whether he ever mentioned a painting, or a carpet, or a poem, or something that was external to the music that was, maybe not an inspiration, but something that prompted his thinking about a musical problem.

DH: I remember he spoke a lot of Aki's playing. He was very inspired by the coloring of her playing. That's what I remember the most.

RF: So you don't have any recollections of his sharing his intention about this piece—what he was trying to do?

DH: That's why I think you should talk with Aki.

RF: I will try to contact Aki, and thank you very much for sharing your time and memories with me.

NOTES

1. The Kronos Quartet premiered *String Quartet II* on December 4, 1983, at the University of Toronto (according to the Feldman Archive at the University of Buffalo).

2. Feldman's *String Quartet II* at tempo has a duration of five to six hours when played straight through without intermissions.

3. That is, a copy of the autograph that Morton Feldman prepared in his own hand, dated September 20, 1985.

4. Aki Takahashi confirmed that these were notational errors and shared the corrections that are on her copy of the score in an email to Ray Fields dated June 30, 2017. On page 29 of the autograph score, first system, second measure, the notes in the piano part are C5-G5-B5-D♭6-F♯6-B6 (with a natural sign). Based on the chord structure for the piano part in this section of the piece (and its many transpositions), the last interval is always a minor 6th. Ms. Takahashi confirmed this and, accordingly, had changed her score so that the last note of the figure is D7(with a natural sign) in place of B6. Similarly, on the same page, second system, seventh measure, the notes in the piano part are A♭4-E♭5-G5-A5 (with a natural sign)-D6-D♭7; Ms. Takahashi had corrected her score so that the last note of the figure is B♭6 instead of D♭7. Finally, in the third system of page 29, fourth measure, the notes in the piano part are A4-E5-G♯5-B♭5-E♭6-A♭6; however, the correct final note is B6 (with a natural sign) instead of A♭6.

Appendix E
Page from Morton Feldman's Sketches for
Piano and String Quartet

Figure App E.1.
Morton Feldman Collection, Paul Sacher Foundation, Basel (used with permission)

Selected Bibliography

Cline, David. *The Graph Music of Morton Feldman*. Cambridge: Cambridge University Press, 2016.

DeLio, Thomas, ed. *The Music of Morton Feldman*. Westport, CT: Greenwood Press, 1996.

DeLio, Thomas. "The Marvelous Illusion: Morton Feldman's *The Viola in My Life (1)* (1970)." *Contemporary Music Review*, Vol. 32, No. 6 (2013), 589–638.

Feldman, Morton. *Morton Feldman: Essays*, ed. Walter Zimmerman. Kerpen: Beginner Press, 1985.

———. *Give My Regards to Eighth Street: Collected Writings of Morton Feldman*, ed. B. H. Friedman. Cambridge, MA: Exact Change, 2000.

———. *Morton Feldman in Middelburg: Words on Music—Lectures and Conversations, Vol. 1*, ed. Raoul Mörchen. Köln: Ed. MusikTexte, 2008.

———. *Morton Feldman in Middelburg: Words on Music—Lectures and Conversations, Vol. 2*, ed. Raoul Mörchen. Köln: Ed. MusikTexte, 2008.

———. *Morton Feldman Says*, ed. Chris Villars. London: Hyphen Press, 2006.

Gagne, C., and Caras, T., "Morton Feldman [interview]." In *Sound Pieces: Interviews with American Composers*. Metuchen, NJ: Scarecrow Press, 1982.

Gelleny, Sharon Ann. "Variation Techniques and Other Theoretical Issues in Morton Feldman's 'Carpet' Compositions." PhD dissertation, State University of New York at Buffalo, 2000.

Hanninen, Dora A. "Feldman, Analysis, Experience." *Twentieth-Century Music*, 2004: 1/2, 225–251.

———. *A Theory of Music Analysis: On Segmentation and Associative Organization*. Rochester: University of Rochester, 2012.

Janello, Mark K. "The Edge of Intelligibility: Late Works of Morton Feldman." PhD dissertation, University of Michigan, 2001.

Johnson, Steven, ed. *The New York Schools of Music and Visual Arts*, ed. Steven Johnson. New York: Routledge, 2002.

Laws, Catherine. "Morton Feldman's *Neither*: A Musical Translation of Beckett's Text." In *Samuel Beckett and Music*, ed. Mary Bryden. New York: Oxford University Press, 1998.

Reich, Steve. *Writings on Music.* Oxford; New York: Oxford University Press, 2002.

Schoenberg, Arnold. *Style and Idea.* New York: Philosophical Library, 1950.

Wolff, Christian. *Occasional Pieces: Writings and Interviews, 1952–2013.* New York: Oxford University Press, 2017.

Yates, Frances A. *The Art of Memory.* London: Bodley Head, 2014.

Index

Page references for figures are italicized.

Abrash, influence of, 6–7
Ames, Paula, 13
Atlantis, 9

Bartók, Bela, 11
Beckett, Samuel, 9,13
Brown, Earle, 5
Busoni, Ferruccio, 3

Cage, John, 5, 7
Carnegie Hall, 5
Coptic Light, 14
Crippled Symmetry, 11, 14, 57
crippled symmetry in Feldman's
 music, *86, 89*

DeLio, Thomas, 2
Dirge in Memory of Thomas Wolfe, 4
Durations 1–5, *9–10*

Feldman, Frances, 3
Feldman, Irving, 3
Flux Quartet, 14
For Christian Wolff, 2
For Frank O'Hara, 9
For John Cage, 2, 11, 14

For Philip Guston, 2
Forte, Allen, 30

Graph notation, 2, 7–9
Guston, Philip, 5, 117

Hanninen, Dora, 14
harmonic, harmonically, use of term,
 34n8
Harrington, David, 34n7;
 interview with, 111

In Search of an Orchestration, 9
Instruments 1–2, 9
Instruments 3, 6, 9
Intersection 1–4, *8*

Johns, Jasper, 5, 13, 117
Johnson, Steven, 13
Jurkowski, Edward, 13

key centers in Feldman's music, 65n7
Kronos Quartet, 12, 20, 33n6, 111

Mitropoulos, Dimitri, 5
Molloy, novel by Samuel Beckett, 13

Music and Arts High School of New York City, 4
Music for Strings, Percussion and Celesta, 11

New York Philharmonic, 5
"Nieuwe Muziek" festival in Middelburg in the Netherlands, 1

O'Hara, Frank, 5
On Time and the Instrumental Factor, 9
oriental rugs, carpets, influence of, 2, 6–7, 116, 117
Out of Last Pieces, 9

Palais de Mari, 14, 33n7
Paynter, Terrence, 13
Piano, 13
Piano and String Quartet:
    recording on YouTube, 33n6
    notational errors, piano, 118n4
    notational issues, strings, 113–117
    tempo, 33–34n7
Piano, Violin, Viola, Cello, 11, 14
Pollock, Jackson, 5
Press, Vera Maurina, 3
Projection 1–5, 8

Rauschenberg, Robert, 1, 5, 7
Reich, Steve, 3, 10
Riegger, Wallingford, 4

Rite of Spring, 10–11
Rothko Chapel, 1, 2, 7, 9, 16n20
Rothko, Mark, 5

Schoenberg, Arnold, 6, 98
Scriabin, Alexander, 3
Shapey, Ralph, *10*
Spring of Chosroes, 13
Stravinsky, Igor, *10*, 65n6
String Quartet, 11, 12, 111
String Quartet II, 6, 11, 12, 34n12, 111–113, 115, 116–117;
    Christian Wolff's analytic liner notes for, 14

Takahashi, Aki, 12, 17n49–50, 20, 33–34n7, 64n3;
    letter to, from Feldman, 103
Third Street Settlement School, 3
Triadic Memories, 13–14, 33n7, 65n7

Viola in My Life, 1, 2, 7, 9
Violin and Orchestra, 11

Webern, Symphony op. 21, 5
Why Patterns, 2, 6–7, 13
Wolff, Christian, 5, 14
Wolpe, Stefan, 4, 5

Varèse, Edgard, 4

York, Wes, 14

About the Author

Ray Fields is a composer, analyst, and researcher. His works are performed at festivals, conferences, sacred settings, public spaces, and online. He studied with Thomas DeLio, Robert Gibson, Mark Edwards Wilson, and Christopher Pavlakis. His preparation for analyzing Morton Feldman's *Piano and String Quartet* included three weeks of study at the Feldman Archive of the Paul Sacher Stiftung in Basel, Switzerland; interviews with David Harrington of the Kronos Quartet and pianist Aki Takahashi, who premiered and recorded the work, as well as other performers of Feldman's music; and cognitive research on the aural experience of the composition itself. He also had a 25-year career as the director of policy and research for the National Assessment Governing Board, a federal agency that reports to the public on the educational achievement of the nation's fourth-, eighth-, and 12th-grade students.

www.ingramcontent.com/pod-product-compliance
Lightning Source LLC
Chambersburg PA
CBHW021852300426
44115CB00005B/130